# The Continuum Guide to Successful Teaching in Higher Education

Manuel Martinez-Pons

**continuum**
NEW YORK • LONDON

**Continuum**

The Tower Building
11 York Road
London SE1 7NX

370 Lexington Avenue
New York
NY 10017–6503

British Library Cataloguing-in-Publication Data
A catalogue record for this book is available from the British Library.

ISBN: 0–8264–6719–9 (hardback), 0–8264–6718–0 (paperback)

Typeset by RefineCatch Limited, Bungay, Suffolk
Printed and bound in Great Britain by
Biddles Ltd, Guildford and King's Lynn

# Contents

# Contents

# Preface

 This book was written as an introduction to instruction in higher education. The work, written as companion to *The Psychology of Teaching and
Learning: A Three-Step Approach* (Martinez-Pons, 2001), concentrates
on the roles instructors and students play in the teaching-learning effort
in the college setting. It takes a three-phase approach to its subject,
dividing the instructional process into three sequentially occurring sets
of activities the instructor undertakes a) before engaging the student in
the teaching-learning effort, b) as he or she and the student engage in the
teaching-learning effort, and c) following engagement. For each phase,
the book integrates work in the literature deemed tenable into one
cohesive frame of reference for thinking about the instructional process
at the college level.

　　　　The book is divided into four parts spanning seven chapters.
Part 1, offering an overview of the present approach to college instruction, consists of two chapters. Chapter 1 presents definitions of key
terms employed throughout the work and discusses the need for a pedagogy of college instruction, and Chapter 2 offers an overview of such a
pedagogy. Part 2, addressing the pre-engagement phase of instruction,
consists of two chapters. Chapter 3 addresses information-gathering as

the instructor prepares to engage the student in the teaching-learning endeavor, and Chapter 4 covers planning of the activities to be carried out in the engagement phase. Part 3, consisting of Chapter 5, addresses the actual engagement of the student in the teaching-learning undertaking. And Part 4, consisting of chapters 6 and 7, covers the post-engagement phase of instruction. Chapter 6 addresses those activities the instructor undertakes to assess the effectiveness of the teaching-learning effort, and Chapter 7 covers the process of remediation on the basis of evaluation findings.

MMP
Brooklyn College, 2002

# PART 1

## OVERVIEW OF THE PROCESS OF COLLEGE INSTRUCTION

The study of instruction in higher education is concerned with issues ranging as far and wide as social processes; administrators' and instructors' capabilities; instructional planning and evaluation, research design, assessment and statistical analysis of assessment data; and student learning readiness and academic achievement. Part 1, consisting of Chapters 1 and 2, provides a background and overview of the present approach to instruction in higher education taking such issues into account.

# Chapter 1

---

# Background

## INTRODUCTION

This chapter provides a conceptual background for the present view of college instruction. First, it presents definitions of key terms used throughout the book; then, it discusses the need for a pedagogy of college teaching.

## DEFINITION OF TERMS

Two terms are used to refer to the major settings within which post-secondary education, as conceptualized here, takes place: *college* and *university*. While in the technical sense the former term is reserved for institutions offering programs leading to the Associate, Bachelor's or Master's degree, the latter is reserved for institutions providing also academic work leading to the Doctorate degree. On the other hand, the term *college* is often used colloquially to refer without distinction to either higher education setting. In this work, the term will be used in the colloquial sense unless, in making a point, the need arises for differentiating between the two settings.

In addition to the distinction in terminology addressing the settings of higher education, a distinction can be drawn between the type of instruction involved in primary and secondary education on the one hand, and instruction involved in higher education on the other. The term *school teaching*, or *school instruction*, will be used in this book to refer to the former; and the term *college teaching*, or *college instruction*, will be used to refer to the latter.

Third, the term *college professor*, or briefly, *professor*, used at length throughout this work, has a technical meaning. It is used in the college setting as shorthand to refer to someone holding the rank of Assistant, Associate, Full, or Distinguished Professor. On the other hand, the term is also used colloquially to refer to technically non-professorial college-teaching ranks such as those of instructor and lecturer. In this book, the term *professor*, or alternately, *instructor*, will be used in the colloquial sense without distinction of rank to refer to anyone who teaches at the college level.

Finally, the term *pedagogy*, also used extensively throughout this work, will be employed to refer to any conceptual framework intended to guide the systematic study of the process of instruction. As will become apparent, a need exists for a pedagogy of college instruction differing in key respects from one addressing instruction at the school level.

## THE NEED FOR A PEDAGOGY OF COLLEGE INSTRUCTION

In the study of teaching, it is important to keep in mind certain fundamental differences that exist between the school and college settings. The distinction is important because it has implications for the goals and methods of instruction attending the two educational settings—and while in the past much effort has been spent on the development of conceptual frameworks for the study of the instruction of children, comparatively little effort has been devoted to address the characteristics and needs of adult students. In fact, whatever theories of adult instruction have been developed have been based on work related to school classroom processes—an approach to a discipline of adult education too lacking in recognition of the complexities of the lives of adults to be of much value in the planning or conduct of college teaching. In the education of adults, only during the past two or three decades has there been any effort exerted to attend to such complexities (Knowles, Holton & Swanson, 1998).

The above observations are generally true, although, as reported by Nel (1990), as far back as a century ago faculty in one American Northwestern university made provisions in their teaching for the life conditions of their adult students by implementing

> policies regarding exemption from general requirements, recognition of experience, special interest classes, correspondence studies, and off-campus and summer educational opportunities, as found in university archives, personal letters, and policy statements. The study is provocative in the sense that few people realize the degree of institutional responsiveness that existed 100 years ago. (p. 1)

Still, recognizing the rarity of this occurrence, the author observed, "The study raised the question of why more progress has not been made" (p. 1).

Differences between the school and college settings presenting a need for a distinct pedagogy of college instruction are discussed in the following pages.

## Differences Between the School and College Settings

There are at least two ways in which schools and colleges differ that call for approaches to instruction distinct in key respects for the two settings. The differences involve the instructors and students who participate in the instructional processes there.

## Differences Between School and College Instructors

Pedagogically important differences between school and college instructors exist in their general educational preparation, in their formal training in teaching methodology, and in the roles they play in their institutions.

### General Educational Preparation

The training of schoolteachers, leading to the Bachelor's or Master's degree, is largely intended to prepare them to perform as practitioners of their craft, as well as to become critical consumers of information about their craft generated by scholars. By contrast, the training of college professors, with few exceptions leading to the doctorate degree, is meant largely to prepare them to perform scholarly work for the generation of new information.

Differences in their general educational preparation have implications for what schoolteachers and college professors do in the classroom. While the former typically convey to their students scholarly information generated by others and translated by others through textbooks into the language of the classroom, the latter are expected to also convey information they themselves generate through their scholarly activities. This condition makes necessary a distinct pedagogy of college teaching that enables professors to translate the work they perform in their fields of specialization into instructional material.

### Formal Pedagogical Training

Although as a rule schoolteachers do not perform original scholarly work, they are in some respects more readily prepared than are college professors to discuss in the classroom information generated by others: while the former receive extensive training in pedagogy as well as in the content areas in which they teach, the latter, unless they undergo some of form of teacher training at the Bachelor's or Master's level, do not. For example, at the time of this writing, at the university in which the present author teaches, teacher education leading to a Bachelor's degree included around 60 hours in the liberal arts and 60 hours in pedagogy; and preparation at the Master's level required around 30 hours beyond the Bachelor's degree, of which around 27 hours were devoted entirely to pedagogical training. Except for those in programs in education, doctoral students, by contrast, were normally trained only in their areas of specialization (e.g., physics, sociology, musicology), receiving little or no formal preparation in pedagogy. At any rate, regardless of the institution involved, in general, other than those in doctoral programs in adult education, whatever pedagogical training doctoral students receive is likely to be oriented toward the education of children.

Since formal training in instruction has not formed part of the curricula followed by doctoral students preparing for college teaching, historically no requirement has been felt for development of a pedagogy of college instruction, as distinct from one of school instruction, that would guide such training—a condition leaving extant a need for a discipline of college teaching taking into account important characteristics of the higher-education setting (Gaff & Pruitt-Logan, 1998; Osgood & York, 1992).

### Roles Teachers and Professors Play in Education

Differences between schoolteachers' and college professors' roles relative to their students and to their institutions have important implications for distinct pedagogies of school and college instruction.

***Roles Relative to Students.*** Schoolteachers primarily help their students to develop basic skills in reading, writing and arithmetic, and the general knowledge they convey to their pupils is elementary, meant to serve as the basis for the acquisition of further fundamental knowledge at later stages of their school work. Teachers' involvement with their charges consists partly of assisting them in developing mental frameworks for beginning of the systematic exploration of their world, and they seek to cultivate in their pupils habits of study, punctuality and compliance with rules that will help them to function as students.

By contrast, college professors typically seek to complete the preparation of their students for independent functioning as adults. They assume that their charges come equipped with the basic mental frameworks necessary for learning (exceptions to this rule are considered cases for remediation), and their work, intended to go beyond the transmission of elementary information, is meant to ultimately provide learners with skills and knowledge that they can apply to their functioning as adults—in the management of their lives, in their participation in the societal decision-making process, and often, in their work.

Thus, college professors begin the education of adults where that of children leaves off, and this work presents a need for a distinct pedagogy of college instruction that goes beyond the educational processes that typify primary and secondary schools.

***Roles Relative to the Institution.*** While schoolteachers are largely expected to comply with policies and procedures formulated by administrators, college professors participate extensively in the identification and development of the curricular goals, policies, and procedures of their institutions. In fact, in the typical college, curricular decisions are made with the advice and consent of a *faculty senate* composed of instructional staff elected to that body. In this way, college professors play central roles in determining what is taught in college—a state of affairs making a distinct pedagogy of college teaching particularly relevant to help guide in the curricular development, implementation and evaluation efforts that occur in higher education.

Thus, differences between instructors in schools and colleges have important implications for a pedagogy of college teaching that differs in key respects from one of school instruction. Differences also exist between school-age and college-age students that call for distinct pedagogies for the two educational settings.

### Differences Between School-Age and College-Age Students

School-age students depend to a large extent on adults for the shelter, sustenance, and general support they need for their welfare and development. In addition, they are expected to comply with rules generated by adults—two of which for children are compulsory school attendance and participation in a typically uniform school curriculum.

While adults too are subject to certain levels of dependency and rule compliance, they in addition exercise degrees of independence (e.g., voluntary participation in education) and self-sufficiency not typical of children—although along with these levels of self-reliance adults, also in contrast with children, are held legally and financially accountable for much of what they do in the course of everyday life. Moreover, adults are instrumental in the generation, distribution, and acquisition of those things necessary for their own as well as for others' well-being—and they play, in addition, a part in the formulation of the rules that govern social conduct. These conditions impose on adult students, in contrast with school age pupils, a worldview and set of life priorities that greatly influence their educational goals and their conduct in pursuit of these goals (for example, they may assign to their schoolwork a role secondary to other social responsibilities such as jobs and homemaking), necessitating a pedagogy of higher education attending to the worldview, life goals, and goal-seeking processes characterizing adult learners (Knowles, Holton & Swanson, 1998).

In summary, differences between instructors in schools and colleges on the one hand, and between students in schools and colleges, on the other, have important implications for pedagogies addressing instruction at these two institutional levels. The remainder of this work is devoted to consideration of key elements of a pedagogy of college instruction.

# Chapter 2

## Overview of a Pedagogy of College Instruction

### INTRODUCTION

C hapter 2 provides an overview of the pedagogy of college instruction described in more detail in subsequent chapters. First, it examines the fields of educational psychology and adult education with a view to garner elements from each discipline that can be integrated into a pedagogy of college teaching. Then, it presents an overview of the process of college instruction integrating principles and theory found in the two fields.

### EDUCATIONAL PSYCHOLOGY AND ADULT EDUCATION THEORY: A CONFLUENCE OF COMPLEMENTARY DISCIPLINES FOR A PEDAGOGY OF COLLEGE INSTRUCTION

#### Educational Psychology

Educational psychology has evolved during the past century into the primary field concerned with the conduct of theory building and research in education. While at first the field was seen as psychology applied to education, according to Davis (1983) the discipline ". . . has assumed an identity of its own and no longer accepts the obsolete psychology-applied-to-education label" (p. 8). The legitimacy of educational psychology today as a discipline in its own right is manifested by its representation as Division 15 (*The Division of Educational Psychology*) in the American Psychological Association.

The discipline of educational psychology is broad, addressing such aspects of education as classroom dynamics, student development, learning processes, motivation, instructional methodology, individual differences, measurement theory, and research methodology (Davis, 1983); and ". . . the study of language and thought, metacognition, discourse structures, strategic instruction, and teacher decision making" (Berliner & Calfee, 1996, p. 7).

Edward L. Thorndike (1874–1949) is credited with foundation of the discipline in the United States with publication of his text *Educational Psychology* in 1903 (Hilgard, 1996), and later with his participation in the establishment of the journal *Educational Psychology*. Hilgard (1996) traced European precursors of Thorndike's work to such workers as Jean Jacques Rousseau (1712–1778) in France, Johann Heinrich Pestalozzi (1746–1827) in Switzerland, Friedrich Froebel (1782–1852) in Germany, and John Locke (1632–1704) in Britain. Hilgard (1996) also cited William James (1842–1910), Granville Stanley Hall (1844–1924) and Charles H. Judd (1873–1946) as precursors of educational psychology in the United States. In modern times, leaders in the field such as Albert Bandura, David Berliner, Dale Schunk, Linn Corno, Lee J. Cronbach, Ernest Hilgard, Frank Pajares, Paul Pintrich, Michael Pressley, and Barry J. Zimmerman are among the many educational psychologists making groundbreaking contributions to the educational enterprise through theory building and research.

Because of its rigorous focus on teaching-learning processes, educational psychology is particularly well equipped to provide the educator with a frame of reference that he or she can use as he or she attempts to formulate a pedagogy of college instruction.

## Possible Reservations Concerning the Role of Educational Psychology in the Education of Adults

Some reservations are possible regarding the breadth and scope of educational psychology in its ability to address key issues involved in the education of adults. First, the field, like psychology in general, has tended to develop in a fragmented manner, so that it is possible for workers specializing in, say, quantitative methods to have limited detailed knowledge of the work performed by workers specializing in, say, cognitive development. In addition, different paradigmatic stances are held by different groups of educational psychologists (for example, the organismic stance of Piagetian scholars *versus* the contextualist position of social cognitivist theorists)—conditions that a college instructor may find daunting as he or she attempts to apply principles and concepts he or she gathers from different compartments of educational psychology in his or her development of instructional methodology.

A second possible reservation concerning educational psychology relative to adult education is the approach that workers in this field have historically taken to theory building. According to Shulman and Quinlan (1996), in the past workers in this area have tended to concentrate on the formulation of grand theories of learning and instruction (for example, the works of Judd, 1916, 1936, on the generality of transfer; and Gagné, 1985, on the general conditions of learning), tending to overlook contextual factors of the learning setting that contribute to the success or failure of the teaching-learning effort. Schulman and Quinlan (1996) argued that teaching effectiveness is dependent on context-specific factors such as knowledge of the content and syntax of the topic being taught, and that therefore educational psychologists must begin taking these situation-specific issues into account in their treatment of learning and instruction.

A third possible reservation regarding educational psychology relative to adult education involves the emphasis of the former on the study of the development of children (Pressley & McCormick, 1995). As already noted, fundamental differences exist between the school and college settings that necessitate a discipline of college instruction going beyond one addressing the instruction of school-age students.

Finally, some writers have argued that there is much that happens in the teaching-learning setting that educational psychology in its present form is not equipped to address. For example, Kallos and Lundgren (1975) posited that of necessity the scientific approach used in this field overlooks important aspects of instruction:

> The reductionism found in current psychological explanations of the teaching-learning process has prevented fuller and more realistic descriptions in which the whole social context of teaching is considered, in terms of rules which govern what happens in classrooms. (p. 111)

## Contribution of Educational Psychology to a Pedagogy of College Teaching

Despite the above possible reservations about educational psychology relative to college teaching, there can be little doubt concerning the pragmatic value for college instruction that methodology in research and theory-building in this field have to offer to a pedagogy of college instruction. First, the work of educational psychologists tends to be highly focused and detailed, adhering to rigorous scientific principles—lending their contributions to education a high level of theoretical credence and heuristic value. Second, the field has steadily evolved, keeping pace with paradigmatic shifts in the way social scientists view human behavior. Examples of this evolution are the contextualist works of such social cognitive theorists as Bandura (1986), Zimmerman and Martinez-Pons (1986), and Zimmerman (1989) on self-efficacy and self-self-regulatory learning behavior, discussed below, departing radically from the mechanistic formulations of behaviorists in explaining and predicting academic achievement; the work of Martinez-Pons (1999) on self-regulated transfer behavior; the work of Ericsson and Charnes (1994) on deliberate practice as a viable alternative to the concept of native ability in explaining performance; and the work of Derry and Lesgold (1998) on task analysis, which, considering the learner as an active participant in the task analysis process, goes beyond the original global, teacher-centered approach of Gagné. These advances in the field enable educational psychology to offer much to the educator attempting to develop a pedagogy of college instruction.

## Adult Education Theory

Probably one of the more comprehensive and influential efforts in the development of adult education as a distinct discipline has been the work of Malcolm Knowles (1970) on what he termed *andragogy*. Knowles adopted the term from Savicevic (1985, 1999) a Yugoslav scholar who espoused a traditional European view of higher education in which two adults interact *"as adults"*, the interplay enabling one to acquire some concept, skill, or disposition. In Knowles' terminology, "andragogy" means "the education of adults", and the term *pedagogy* is restricted to mean "the education of children". Knowles' andragogical "technology", in his view different from "pedagogical" methods, can be summarized in terms of three major sets of activities:

1. Development of instructional objectives on the basis of student needs and interests
2. Collaboration between instructor and student in the identification of instructional content, procedures, and resources in pursuit of instructional objectives
3. Continual evaluation and modification of instructional procedures.

## Reservations Concerning Andragogy

A number of reservations can be noted concerning the work of Knowles as it relates to college instruction. First, Knowles' original work was devoted to adult education in "informal" environments (that is, environments outside the college setting) where, in Knowles' view, students should determine the content and form of instruction. But generalization of this andragogical principle to the college classroom would tend to overlook professional and institutional exigencies that transcend the outlook of students regarding the goals and methods of higher education. The substance and standards of disciplines covered in college curricula are determined by professional organizations, and institutions of higher learning strive to adhere to such professional concerns in their curricular programs. While in the latter phases of their college education students can begin to have some input, adhering to such guidelines, into the content and form of college instruction, in the beginning the informed contribution they can make in this regard cannot be expected to be extensive.

A second reservation concerning Knowles' work relative to college instruction involves his conceptualization of pedagogy. It would appear that he overstated his case in his characterization of pedagogy exclusively in terms of the education of children, since, in fact, the laws of learning are the same for adults in college as they are for school-age students. For example, behavioral schedules of reinforcement (Skinner, 1968) apply with equal force to the two groups: the social mechanism through which people learn and become proficient at some task (Bandura, 1980; Zimmerman, 1999) is the same for adults as it is for children, and information-processing aspects of learning (Schunk, 1991) apply to any learner regardless of age.

In a related matter, a third reservation concerning Knowles' work relative to college instruction involves his proposed pedagogy-andragogy dichotomy. According to Houle (1974) and Kidd (1980), viewing the two approaches as mutually exclusive is misleading, since learning for adults as well as for children moves seamlessly between the prescriptive mode Knowles said to characterize school teaching and the collaborative mode he envisioned for adult education. In fact, according to Mohring (1989), the etymological precision of the term *andragogy* is questionable:

> The use of the term "andragogy" to mean education of adults and the term "pedagogy" to mean education of children is etymologically inaccurate. Although pedagogy derives from "pais," meaning child, from antiquity pedagogy also has stood for education in general— without reference to learners' ages. (p. 1)

## Contributions of Adult Education Theory to a Discipline of College Teaching

Despite the above reservations concerning Knowles' approach to the education of adults, there can be little doubt concerning the pragmatic value for college instruction of some of the tenets of his work. The notion is important that along with self-sufficiency and multiple social responsibilities comes a worldview with implications for the educational goals adults set for themselves and for the way in which they pursue these goals. In addition, Knowles' "technology" of adult education seems indispensable for effective instruction, regardless of the age of the student at hand. In fact, it is interesting that, as noted by Carré (1998), principles of adult education, which evolved in reaction against the perceived rigid, mechanical, "one size fits all" approach of traditional school instruction, have "trickled down" to the school level, so that at present many of these tenets underlie childhood instruction as well as adult education.

## Integration of Principles of Educational Psychology and Adult Education Into a Pedagogy of College Instruction

Arguing for an integration of traditional and adult-education principles for a science of adult instruction, Tice (1997) stated,

> In the conceptual debate over the appropriate methods for adult learning, both those who think learning only occurs at the feet of the master and those who think that adults should be totally self-directed are right to an extent. A balance is needed, considering the age . . . and desired outcomes of the student. (p. 18)

In fact, toward this end, a movement has already begun to integrate aspects of the disciplines of educational psychology and adult education. Termed *adult educational psychology* (Smith & Pourchot, 1998), the proposed field ". . . is primarily concerned with understanding the relationship of learning and development and the ways in which learning contributes to adult life-span development" (p. 260). According to Smith and Pourchot (1998), adult educational psychology is based on the premises that a) a connection exists between learning in adulthood and life-span development, b) new scientific methods should be developed to study this relationship, c) the primary focus of adult educational psychology should be the educational setting, and d) adult educational psychology, although interfacing significantly with adult education, remains a distinct discipline in its own right.

Notwithstanding the fact that adult educational psychology is still in its infancy and that it is thus subject to the challenges faced by any fledgling discipline (for example, in this case, according to Smith and Pourchot, possible resistance from successful adult educators who see little need for the new field), its foundation, with publication of *Adult Learning and Development: Perspectives From Educational Psychology* (Smith & Pourchot, 1998), points to the recognized need for an integration of aspects of educational psychology and adult education to address key issues regarding the education of adults.

In what follows, the three elements extracted above from Knowles' work on adult education (attention to student concerns in the development of instructional objectives, instructor-student collaboration in designing instructional content, continual evaluation of instructional effectiveness) are incorporated into a model of college instruction, and, following Knowles, the work described below takes into account the life circumstances of adult learners in its treatment of instructional planning. At the same time, the present work departs from Knowles' andragogical stance in three key respects. First, following Houle (1974), Kidd (1980), and Tice (1997), it takes a contextualist approach to college teaching, recognizing the roles played by prescriptive as well as by collaborative instruction as functions of the varying conditions under which college teaching takes place. Second, the framework considers the level of influence on the content of instruction exerted by key individuals in addition to the student. Third, following Mohring (1989), this approach uses the term "pedagogy" to refer to any conceptual framework employed to guide instruction, regardless of the age of the students involved.

In addition to the use of adult-education principles for its general framework, the present work employs concepts, theory, research design, and research findings from the field of educational psychology as bases for the methodology in needs assessment, diagnosis, and curricular development and evaluation in college instruction described in the following chapters. Regarding the budding field of adult educational psychology (Smith & Pourchot, 1998) and its relevance to the present work, while that field addresses the education of adults regardless of the instructional setting, the present effort integrates principles of adult education and educational psychology specifically for the treatment of college instruction.

Finally, following Kallos and Lundgren (1975), such instruction-related issues as resource allocation and college curricular decision-making processes, considered here to lie outside the scopes of adult education and educational psychology, are deemed important topics for consideration in instructional planning, and the present approach takes into account their role in instruction in the context of the college setting.

## THE CONTEXTS AND MODES OF COLLEGE INSTRUCTION

As already noted, college instruction is characterized by factors that differentiate it in key respects from that of school instruction—and in discussing it, it is advantageous to consider the contexts of higher education within which it takes place and the modes of instruction through which it occurs.

### The Context of College Instruction

The context of college teaching involves an institutional setting within which instruction takes place, a typical time frame within which program completion occurs, and a certain mode of instructor-student interaction through which the teaching-learning effort is conducted. Variation in these conditions of higher education necessitates adjustments in the way college instruction is planned and executed.

### Institutional Setting

Differences between institutional settings can influence the manner in which college instruction is conducted. For present purposes, there are five major, overlapping, institutional settings within which college instruction takes place: the community college, the technical college, the liberal arts college, the school of arts and sciences, and the professional school (in some institutions, the terms *school* and *college* can be interchanged).

## Time Frame

In addition to its institutional setting, the context of college instruction involves a time frame, varying as a function of setting, within which program completion typically occurs—a time frame with implications for the way instruction is structured. Typically, community colleges offer two-year programs leading to the Associate degree; technical colleges offer two- and four-year programs leading to the Associate and Bachelor's degrees, respectively; liberal arts colleges offer two-, four-, and five-to-six-year programs leading respectively to the Associate, Bachelor's and Master's degrees; schools of arts and sciences offer four-, five-to-six, and six-plus-year programs leading to the Bachelor's, Master's and Doctorate degrees, respectively; and professional schools offer five-to-six- and six-plus-year programs leading respectively to the Master's and Doctorate degrees. The relevance of these time frames for instruction is that the longer the period assigned for program completion, the broader the range of instructional methods the educator can attempt in his or her work with specific groups of students. Such instructional methods are discussed below.

## The Levels of College Instruction

In addition to its setting and time frame, the college context involves a level of instruction that varies as a function of time frame and setting. For the Associate and Bachelor's degrees, the level of instruction can be considered *basic* in the sense that it seeks to provide students with an elementary understanding of procedures and concepts related to any number of subjects, presenting learners with a foundation for subsequent college study. It also seeks to provide students with ways they can use to critically incorporate some of what they learn into their view of the world around them as well as into aspects of their social functioning. While the incorporation of learned material into aspects of an adult's work can occur in certain undergraduate programs—for example, X-ray technician and practical nursing at the Associate level, and civil engineering and teacher education at the Bachelors level—much undergraduate work takes a liberal arts orientation designed to serve as general foundation for further study, and for some application by students to the management of various areas of their lives. In any case, the information conveyed at the undergraduate level is fundamental when compared to that offered in master's and doctoral programs.

At the Master's level, a great deal of attention is devoted to a single discipline (e.g., school psychology), enabling participating students to develop skills (for example, skills in individual intelligence testing for school psychologists) that they can apply to the practice of their craft. Students at this level are also helped in their development of information-gathering skills (for example, skills in reading, interpreting, and evaluating works found in the professional literature) that they can use to keep abreast of developments in their fields. In this sense, Master's work can be considered to be applied—standing at an intermediate level between the broad fundamental work typical of undergraduate programs and the highest level of instruction comprising doctoral training.

At the doctoral level, a great deal of attention is also devoted to a single field of study, but with an end in mind to provide students with the skills necessary to further their craft through research and theory-building activities. In this sense, work at the doctoral level can be considered advanced in that it moves beyond application of existing knowledge to the generation of new information.

Differences between college contexts have much to do with the manner in which instruction takes place in higher education since, as a rule, the shorter the time period for program completion (and typically, the more basic the information conveyed), the higher the level of prescriptive instruction and the lower the degree of collaborative interaction likely to occur between instructor and student; conversely, the longer the time period for program completion (and typically, the more advanced the instruction as time progresses), the greater the opportunity for instructor-student collaboration in the pursuit of instructional objectives.

It should be noted that the levels of instruction referred to above have to do with the *opportunity* for providing training involving orientation (undergraduate programs), application (master's programs), and information generation (doctoral programs) rather than necessarily with the actual provision of these forms of training. It is possible for instruction in a given Master's class to be only more of the same orientation material presented at the undergraduate level, or for instruction in a given doctoral class to be only more of the same training in application ideally found at the Master's level. What is important is the opportunity for the appropriate level of instruction afforded by the time frame and the readiness level of the students involved—and the question related to this matter is whether the instructor takes advantage of this opportunity. These issues have important implications for the mode of instruction employed in college.

## The Modes of College Instruction

A distinction can be drawn between two major modes of college teaching. One involves a directive, prescriptive approach to the task on the instructor's part, with little or no input from students concerning the objectives or methodology of the teaching-learning effort. This mode, geared to the transmission of sizeable amounts of introductory information to large audiences, is usual in the early college years, during a time when learners are typically in the initial phases in their development of skills for successful functioning as college students. In this mode of instruction, the educator a) introduces the topic at hand; b) reviews the instructional objectives and offers a preview of the activities to follow; c) provides exposure to the material through whatever means (readings, lectures, etc.) he or she deems appropriate; d) allows for questions and answers for clarification; e) allows students to demonstrate their level of mastery of the material during instruction and provides them with feedback as necessary to enable them to improve their mastery; and f) provides them with an opportunity to practice the transfer of acquired material to situations or tasks different from those involved in the original effort. Martinez-Pons (2001) describes in detail this approach to instruction.

The second mode of college instruction, the ultimate distinguishing hallmark of college teaching, associated with small classes, is collaborative in nature and involves a combination of class seminar and dialogue between instructor and student, with the dialogue culminating at the highest levels with the generation of the new information that characterizes the thesis and dissertation. This instructional mode is discussed in Chapter 4.

It should be noted that the relation between the prescriptive and collaborative modes of instruction is neither quantitative, in the sense of a continuum ranging between the two, nor one of mutual exclusivity. Rather, it is best seen as a) *qualitative*, in that each involves a unique form of instruction not true of the other; b) *complementary*, in that at any point in the process of instruction each serves a necessary function that the other cannot serve; and c) *proportional*, in that utilization of one increases in proportion, in fact inversely, to utilization of the other throughout the educational process—although typically, each mode is asymptotic at its lowest level of utilization in that it is seldom completely excluded from the instructional process.

It should also be noted that the above discussion of instructional modalities has to do with the relative *opportunity* for collaborative *vs.* prescriptive work afforded by the various levels of college teaching, rather than necessarily with their actual use, since it is possible for instruction conducted at the undergraduate level to involve greater instructor-student collaboration than instruction conducted at the doctoral level. What is important is the instructor's use of the opportunity for the optimal combination of the prescriptive and collaborative modes afforded by the circumstances at hand.

| Context | | | | |
|---|---|---|---|---|
| | **Academic Degree and Time Frame** | | | |
| **Setting** | Associate 2 Years | Bachelors 4 Years | Masters 5–6 Years | Doctorate 6+ Years |
| Community College | x | | | |
| Technical College | x | x | | |
| Liberal Arts College | x | x | x | |
| School of Arts and Sciences | | x | x | x |
| Professional School | | | x | x |
| **Instructional Level** | *Basic* | | *Intermediate* | *Advanced* |

| | |
|---|---|
| **Instructional Mode** | Prescriptive |
| | Collaborative |
| **Typical Class Size** | Large.........................................................................Small |

**Figure 2.1. Context and Modes of College Instruction**

       Figure 2.1 depicts relations that exist between the context (setting, time frame, and instructional level) and modes of college instruction. As the setting moves beyond that of the community college, the time frame for program completion and the instructional level tend to increase, the degree of dialogue and collaboration between instructor and student also tends to increase (in fact, the increase can be dramatic in the latter years of Bachelor's programs in first-tier colleges requiring a senior thesis), and the level of prescriptive, instructor-to-student exposition as well as class size tend to decrease in inverse proportion to that of collaboration.

       Thus, the mode which college instruction takes is a function of the higher-learning context in which it occurs. This mode can be prescriptive, involving goals and methods determined outside of the student's control; or it can be collaborative, in inverse proportion to prescriptive interaction, involving extensive student input into the goals of instruction and the methods used in pursuit of these goals.

Throughout the rest of this work, a high degree of collaboration between educator and student will be assumed in discussing the process of college instruction. Conditions creating a demand for higher levels of prescriptive teaching will be treated as cases to be approached in such a way as to expedite transition toward the higher levels of instruction involving collaborative activities by instructor and students.

Regardless of the context or instructional mode involved, it is useful to think of college teaching in terms of phases through which the effort takes place. The following paragraphs introduce a frame of reference for thinking about the process of college instruction in terms of such phases.

## THE PHASES OF COLLEGE INSTRUCTION

The instructional endeavor can be thought of as a three-phase process: the *pre-engagement* phase, the *engagement* phase and the *post-engagement* phase. The activities involved in each of these phases are summarized in Figure 2.2, adapted from Martinez-Pons (2001).

### The Pre-Engagement Phase of College Instruction

The pre-engagement phase of college instruction involves those tasks the educator performs in preparation to engage the student in the teaching-learning effort. As shown in Figure 2.2, elements of this phase of the instructional process include *needs assessment, diagnostic activities, development of instructional objectives* and *instructional module development*.

### The Engagement Phase of College Instruction

In the engagement phase of college instruction, the educator involves the student in the teaching-learning effort. As shown in Figure 2.2, elements of this phase of the instructional process include *situational assessment, module implementation, formative evaluation* and *crisis intervention*.

### The Post-Engagement Phase of College Instruction

In the post-engagement phase of college instruction, the educator assesses the effectiveness of the teaching-learning effort he or she has just completed, and he or she makes corrections as necessary to ensure the

| PRE-ENGAGEMENT | ENGAGEMENT | POST-ENGAGEMENT |
|---|---|---|
| **Needs Assessment** | **Situational Assessment and Final Module Adjustments** | **Summative Evaluation** |
| **Diagnostics** | Physical environment | Targets |
| Student learning readiness | Materials | Student performance |
| Instructor teaching readiness | Students | Instructor performance |
|  | Institutional support | School support |
| **Instructional Objectives and** |  | Methodology |
| **Task Analysis** | **Module Implementation** | Sources |
| Domains | Execution | Administrators |
| Cognitive | Social-cognitive processes | Students |
| Affective | Modeling | Instructors |
| Psychomotor | Encouragement | Assessment methods |
|  | Facilitation | Observations |
| **Test Development/Selection** | Rewards | Tests |
| Validity, reliability |  | Questionnaires |
| Types of tests | **Formative Evaluation and** | Consultants |
| Teacher-made vs published | **Corrective Activity** | Critical incident reports |
| Norm- vs. criterion-referenced | Targets |  |
| Objectives-related test properties | Student performance | **Remediation** |
| Assessment research design | Instructor performance | Student performance |
|  | Institutional support | Instructor performance |
| **Pre-Testing and Grouping** | Assessment methods | Institutional support |
|  | Observations | Methodological procedures |
| **Instructional Module** | Tests and quizzes | Pre-engagement |
| **Development and Debugging** | Consultations | Engagement |
| Module structure | Critical incident reports | Post-engagement |
| Lower level: Delivery |  |  |
| Introduction |  |  |
| Demonstration/description |  |  |
| Questions and answers |  |  |
| Student enactment |  |  |
| Feedback and corrective |  |  |
| action |  |  |
| Summary |  |  |
| Higher Level: Collaboration |  |  |
| Seminar and topic survey |  |  |
| Instructor-student dialogue |  |  |
| and course project |  |  |

**Figure 2.2. The Phases of College Instruction.** Adapted from Martinez-Pons (2001).

success of future attempts in the same direction. As shown in Figure 2.2, elements of this phase of the instructional process include *summative evaluation, student remediation* and *methodological revisions.*

Thus, in the pre-engagement phase of college instruction, the educator prepares to engage the student in the teaching-learning effort; in the engagement phase, the educator involves the student in this process; and in the post-engagement phase the educator looks back and assesses the success of the effort, and takes corrective action to improve the likelihood of success in subsequent efforts.

Three questions can be posed for each of the three phases of instruction introduced above:

1. How is each phase best conceptualized at the college level?
2. How relevant is each phase to the success of the college teaching-learning effort?
3. What are areas of each phase in need of theoretical elaboration or further research?

The fields of adult education and educational psychology have much to say about the activities that take place in each of the major phases of college instruction.

## SUMMARY

In summary, college instruction differs in key respects from instruction at the school level. Differences between school and college instructors and between school and college students have important implications for a need for a pedagogy of college instruction. In addition, whether the form instruction takes is prescriptive or collaborative depends on the context in which college instruction takes place.

Educational psychology and adult education are two fields with much to contribute to a discipline of college instruction. Educational psychology is that field which specializes in exploring, through scientific research, the psychological, social and systemic dynamics involved in the three phases of college instruction. Adult education is that field of education concerned with the instruction of adults.

The college instructional process can be divided into three phases: The pre-engagement phase, in which the instructor prepares to interact with the student in the teaching-learning effort; the engagement phase, in which the instructor involves the student in the teaching-learning enterprise; and the post-engagement phase, in which the instructor assesses the success of the teaching-learning effort following its completion.

Figure 2.2 offers an overview of the activities involved in each phase of the instructional process. The rest of this work is devoted to an exploration of the elements appearing in Figure 2.2. For each element, the work discusses a) the theoretical work that has been used to describe it, b) the research that has been conducted in support of theory addressing it, c) issues revolving around the area, and d) significance of the area for the success of the instructional enterprise. The following pages begin this exploration by examining the pre-engagement phase of college instruction.

# PART 2

# THE PRE-ENGAGEMENT PHASE OF COLLEGE INSTRUCTION

In the pre-engagement phase college instruction, the educator prepares to enable the student to acquire the information, skills or dispositions that will constitute the objectives of the teaching-learning effort.

The pre-engagement phase of college instruction can be divided into two facets: a) determination of the needs to be addressed through the teaching-learning effort, and determination of student and instructor characteristics relevant to the goals of instruction; and b) development of the instructional activities that will be used to enable students to reach the goals of instruction. Chapter 3 addresses the information-gathering facet of the pre-engagement phase of college instruction, and Chapter 4 addresses the preparation of instructional activities.

# Chapter 3

---

# Information Gathering

## INTRODUCTION

Chapter 3 discusses that facet of college teaching during which the instructor gathers information in preparation for the planning of the teaching-learning effort. There are two sets of information the instructor seeks at this point: through the process of *needs assessment*, he or she seeks information about what the instructional effort is to involve; and through *diagnostic activities*, he or she seeks information about the participants in the teaching-learning effort that may be relevant for the planning of instruction.

## NEEDS ASSESSMENT

It was argued in Chapter 2 that the work involved in college instruction is meant to enable students to acquire information, skills, and dispositions that they can use in the management of their lives, in the performance of aspects of their jobs, and in their participation in the societal decision-making process. In the present stance, needs assessment addresses the general question of what the work is to entail. Persons in addition to the instructor often have something to say about the way in which this question is answered.

### Concerns Expressed by Stakeholders Regarding the Content of Instruction

In the college setting, there are typically three groups of stakeholders or persons with opinions about what the content of instruction should be—and often, with concerns about how instruction should be conducted: administrators; instructional staff, or faculty members; and students (whatever impact that groups outside the college setting have on the content of instruction, they usually exert it through their influence on any of the three stakeholder groups found within the institution).

The level of influence each stakeholder group directly exerts on the content of instruction can vary across group, across time period, and across institution. While under certain conditions students can exert a great deal of influence in this regard (witness the sway students held on policy making in many universities during the late 1960s and early 1970s), under other circumstances administrators can exert a particularly strong influence (witness the impact of university administrations on the educational standards movement of the 1990s) – and at others, the influence of faculty can be especially pronounced, as often happens in institutional settings with strong faculty organizations.

Figure 3.1 shows relations that exist between efforts devoted to needs identified by college administrators, faculty members, and students. In area *a*, only needs expressed by administrators are addressed through the instructional effort; in area *b*, only concerns are addressed expressed by faculty; and in area *c*, only needs expressed by students are attended to. Intersections between areas show concerns common to the parties involved. For any intersection, the greater the overlap, the greater the commonality among the concerns expressed by the stakeholder groups. The larger the number of areas covered for each group, the greater the degree of satisfaction with the content of instruction the group can be expected to express.

Two questions can be posed regarding the conditions depicted in Figure 3.1: first, how are stakeholders' concerns to be identified through the needs-assessment effort? And second, having identified these concerns, to what degree is the instructor to attend to each area represented in this figure? As conceptualized here, it is the specific task of needs assessment to address these questions.

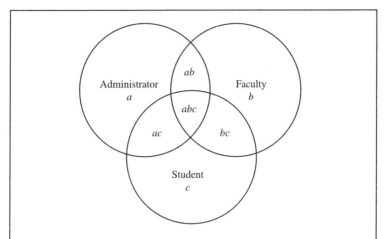

**Figure 3.1. Relationships Among Efforts Devoted to Needs Identified by the Administrators, Students, and Faculty**

## Needs-Assessment Methodology

A number of needs-assessment methods exist. Two approaches, based on principles of *grounded theory research* (see Appendix A for a discussion of grounded theory), will be discussed in the following pages: the *Delphi Procedure*, developed by Norman Dalkey and Olaf Helmer (Lang, 1998); and the *Alpha Method*, developed by the present author.

### The Delphi Procedure

The Delphi procedure is designed to enable the educator to identify positions held by stakeholders regarding the goals of education. It is conducted in four steps:

1. Formation of a panel of stakeholders whose positions the investigator will use as the foundation for planning
2. Elicitation of stakeholder opinions, through structured questionnaires or unstructured, open-ended focus-group interviews regarding the issues of interest
3. Development of a more focused questionnaire on the basis of the qualitative information generated in Step 2
4. Use of the questionnaire developed in Step 3 to elicit more focused information from the panel.

The educator repeats steps 2 through 4 until he or she arrives at a cohesive interpretation of the participants' concerns. Martinez-Pons (2001) offers an example of an adaptation of the Delphi Procedure to a needs assessment conducted at the elementary-school level.

The Delphi Procedure works well for the identification of educational needs. The college instructor deciding which needs to address in his or her classroom for a given course is, however, often faced with limitations in time and resources that impact on his or her instructional planning. This issue requires a method that goes beyond needs identification alone. It requires in addition an approach that enables the instructor to identify those concerns that can actually be addressed, and to predict the level of stakeholder satisfaction likely given the topics the educator selects for instruction. The importance of the last requirement is that, depending on their influence within an institution of higher learning, stakeholders' support or resistance (budgetary backing or opposition by administrators; approval or disapproval by a faculty curriculum review committee; course recommendation for or against, or participation or avoidance by, students) can have much to do with the viability or success of an instructional undertaking—and such support can vary as a function of the degree of the stakeholders' satisfaction with the content of instruction. The following approach, termed here the *Alpha Method*, is designed to enable the college instructor to address these issues.

**The Alpha Method**

This author designed the Alpha Method to provide the following information to the college instructor planning the teaching-learning effort: a) information that he or she can use to select concerns expressed by stakeholders for inclusion in the instructional effort, and b) information about the likely level of stakeholder support of or resistance to the instructional undertaking.

A key element of the Alpha Method is the concept of *stakeholder press (SP)*, defined as the interaction between a person's stance regarding inclusion or exclusion of some topic in the instructional effort, and his or her capacity for influencing the viability or success of the instructional undertaking.

A second key element of the Alpha Method is the concept of *stakeholder thrust (ST)*, defined as the effective support of a stakeholder in favor of the instructional effort given the content of instruction, the value the stakeholder places on the instructional content, and the influence he or she can exert regarding the viability or success of the instructional effort.

A third key feature of the Alpha Method is the concept of *stakeholder resistance*, or the effective opposition a stakeholder is likely to present to the instructional effort given the content of instruction, the negative value the stakeholder has ascribed to parts of this content, and the influence that he or she can bring to bear on the viability or success of the instructional effort.

The Alpha Method is conducted in six phases:

1. Stakeholder identification
2. Identification of stakeholder concerns
3. Calculation of stakeholder press
4. Selection of stakeholder concerns to address through the instructional effort
5. Determination of stakeholder thrust for the viability or success of the instructional effort
6. Determination of stakeholder resistance to the instructional effort.

Appendix B describes in detail the six phases of the Alpha Method. There, in a fictitious example used for the purpose of illustration, an instructor conducts a needs assessment for a scheduled course in American history. While in Phase 1 he discovers nine topics in American history that stakeholders (administrators, faculty, and students) feel the course should address, in Phase 4 he discovers that he can address only four of these concerns due to time and resource constraints; and in Phase 5 he finds that the thrust stakeholders are likely to provide for the viability or success of the instructional effort is 21 percent of the highest possible thrust for administrators, 12 percent of the highest possible thrust for faculty, and 9 percent of the highest possible thrust for students. Moreover, in Phase 6 he finds that stakeholder administrators are likely to exert 7 percent of their maximum possible resistance to the instructional effort.

The Alpha Method (AM) departs from the approach of the Delphi Procedure in three major respects. First, it does so in that AM takes into account the level of influence stakeholders can bring to bear on instruction; second, it departs from the Delphi Procedure in that it takes into account time and resource constraints that may limit the content of instruction; and third, it departs from the Delphi Procedure in that AM provides information about the likely satisfaction of stakeholder press given the form instruction takes—and its possible implications for the viability or success of the instructional effort.

The Alpha Method departs also from Knowles' andragogical

formulation (see Chapter 2 for a discussion of Knowles' work) in that, while that author envisioned the student as having the principal voice in determining instructional content, the Alpha Method recognizes that at least two parties (i.e., administrators and faculty members) in addition to students have a stake in what takes place in the instructional process—and that the influence each party brings to bear on the instructional effort can vary from one situation to another.

Having selected the content of the instructional effort at hand through needs-assessment activities, the educator can proceed to ascertain the level of readiness of participants to undertake the teaching-learning effort. This facet of the pre-engagement phase of instruction is termed *diagnostics*.

## DIAGNOSTICS

Diagnostics is that set of procedures employed to determine the degree to which students and instructor are prepared to undertake the teaching-learning effort.

### Information About the Student's Preparation to Undertake the Instructional Effort

Two sets of behavioral processes play important roles in the likelihood that an adult student will benefit from the teaching-learning effort: personal processes involving psychological functioning and the management of often conflicting social responsibilities; and academic processes involving preparation for, participation in, and capitalization on the teaching-learning effort. The level of self-regulation the student brings to bear on these processes constitutes his or her learning readiness; in what follows, the two sets of processes will be described following a discussion of the self-regulation concept.

### Self-Regulation

Zimmerman (1989) described a self-regulated student as one who is motivated to accomplish some task, sets realistic goals for himself or herself relative to the task, uses specific activities to pursue these goals, self-monitors to check for strategy effectiveness, and adjusts his or her strategy-usage behavior as necessary to ensure the likelihood of success. Zimmerman and Martinez-Pons (1986) reported differentiating with 90 percent accuracy between high-achieving and average high school students on the basis of specific strategies the students reported using in their schoolwork.

While interest in academic self-regulation has focused mainly on primary and secondary school students, researchers have begun examining aspects of self-regulatory learning among college students as well (see for example Archer, Cantwell & Bourke, 1999; Barnett, 2000; Ley & Young, 1998; Schapiro & Livingston, 2000; Schunk, 1991; Strage, 1998)—although the work with adult learners so far has been restricted to a narrow range of study skills. In preparation for a discussion of the relation of self-regulation with psychological functioning as part of learning readiness in college students, the present author examined self-reports of 40 students in a Master's program in a large urban university concerning the following attributes: emotional self-regulation; academic self-regulation; mental efficiency, or intelligence; and academic performance. (Descriptions of the instruments the author used to assess these attributes appear in Appendices D, E, and F, respectively.) The researcher used path analysis (see Appendix A for a discussion of path analysis) to examine the relations among the variables of interest. The results of the analysis appear in Figure 3.2.

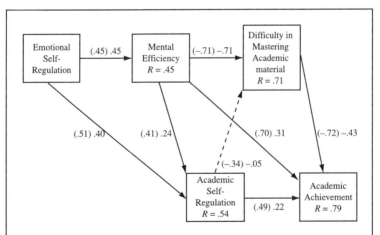

**Figure 3.2. Path Analysis of the Relations among Emotional Self-Regualtion, Academic Self-Regulation, Mental Efficiency, and Academic Achievement in Graduate Students.** All linkage-related coefficients are statistically significant beyond the .05 level. The dashed linkage shows that the effect at hand was spurious, confounded by that of *mental efficiency.*

Figure 3.2 displays raw correlation coefficients, enclosed in parentheses, between linked variables; and direct effects or path coefficients, without parentheses, showing the correlations after the effects of other variables in the model have been statistically controlled. As shown in Figure 3.2, a correlation of $r = .49$, p $< .05$, emerged between *academic self-regulation* and *academic achievement*, decreasing to a direct effect of .22 when the confounding roles of *mental efficiency*, described below, and *difficulty in mastering academic material* were statistically controlled. These outcomes indicate that academic self-regulation plays an important role in the scholastic achievement of adult learners – and that assessment of academic self-regulation is therefore an important aspect of the diagnosis of the learning readiness of college students. Other results appearing in Figure 3.2 will be addressed throughout the remainder of this discussion of student learning readiness.

**Personal Processes**

**Psychological Functioning.** Two aspects of psychological functioning are of special concern regarding the learning readiness of college students: intelligence, or mental efficiency; and emotional soundness.

*Intelligence.* It seems reasonable to expect that a student's mental capacity, or intelligence, will influence his or her readiness to benefit from the teaching-learning effort. Exploration of this matter, however, has been problematic because of the way in which theorists have historically tended to approach the issue. One problem has been the fact that workers in this field have tended to use correlational methodology through which they have factor-analyzed scores on any number of mental tasks to "discover" the mental phenomenon underlying performance on intelligence tests. This approach, although useful in some respects, nevertheless lacks theoretical as well as heuristic power (Jensen, 1985), limiting its usefulness for the diagnosis or promotion of student learning readiness (Bolig & Day, 1993).

In an attempt to address this issue, this author (Martinez-Pons, 1998) used grounded theory methodology (see Appendix A for a discussion of grounded theory) to work out a model of intelligence with a measure of theoretical and heuristic power for educators. He identified three quantifiable behavioral processes comprising mental ability: the speed with which an individual masters new material, the length of time he or she effectively retains mastery, and the extent to which he or she can utilize the material. Figure 3.3 displays this three-component model of intelligence. Since the model addresses what is essentially the

| Component | Performance Dimensions | | Summary |
|---|---|---|---|
| | Amount | Time | |
| Acquisition | How much material is learned | How long it takes to master the material | How much material is learned within a given period of time |
| Retention | How much material is retained | How long the material is retained | How much material is retained over a given period of time |
| Utilization | How extensively the retained material is used | How quickly the retained material is used | How much new information is generated within a given period of time |

**Figure 3.3. Three-Component Model of Intelligence or Mental Efficiency.** From Martinez-Pons (1998).

efficiency with which a person acquires new information, retains it for later use, and utilizes it, this author has begun using the term *mental efficiency* in lieu of the controversial term *intelligence* to refer to the phenomenon in question.

Arguing that traditional standardized tests of intelligence— that is, IQ tests—Wechsler Preschool and Primary School Scale of Intelligence (WPPSI) fail to provide the type of information needed to help in the planning of instruction, Bolig and Day (1993) proposed their *Dynamic Assessment of Giftedness (DAG)* test as a viable alternative. A key feature of the *DAG* is its measurement of training responsiveness, involving what is essentially speed of acquisition, effectiveness of retention and extent of utilization. They reported success in their use of the procedure to address the educational needs of gifted elementary school students, and there seems to be no reason to assume that the methodology cannot be profitably used with students in the college setting as well.

*Relevance of Mental Efficiency to Student Learning Readiness.* Although controversial because of the way in which it has been described and assessed, it is clear that intelligence is a construct with relevance for the likelihood that a student will benefit from instruction. First, it is a construct distinct from but highly predictive of academic achievement. Using a sample of 70 elementary school students, Martinez-Pons (1998) found a correlation of .53 between a factor comprised of acquisition, retention and utilization performance scores and a separate factor comprised of scores on standardized tests of mathematics and reading comprehension. Moreover, as shown in Figure 3.2, for a sample of 40 students in a Master's program, correlations of self-reports of *mental efficiency* emerged with *academic self-regulation* ($r = .41$, $p < .05$, decreasing to .24 when the confounding effect of *emotional self-regulation* was statistically controlled), *difficulty in mastering academic material* (*DMAM*; $r = -.71$, $p < .05$), and *academic achievement* (*Total Effect* = .70; $r = .70$, $p < .05$, decreasing to .31 when the mediating effect of *DMAM* was statistically controlled). In addition to its demonstrable relation to academic performance, when seen as acquisition, retention and utilization efficiency, this conceptualization of intelligence would seem to have intuitive appeal for educators.

Finally, researchers have demonstrated that acquisition, retention, and utilization performance can be improved. Ericsson and Charnes (1994) have shown deliberate practice that, far from being innate, talent is largely a function of practice in the development of a particular skill, and there is no reason to assume that practice cannot have a significant impact on mental ability defined as acquisition, retention and utilization performance. In fact, Webster (1981), and Biehler and Snowman (1982) used attention-getting devices to improve student sensory register functions, rehearsal and chunking techniques to improve short-term memory, and imagery and verbal encoding to improve long-term memory. And Jampole (1990), through his work on higher thinking skills, showed that it is possible to raise the extent to which students can utilize previously mastered material in original ways.

For these reasons, in the view of the present writer, the continuing interest in the topic of intelligence has merit—and when seen as mental efficiency in the form of acquisition, retention and utilization performance, diagnostic targeting as the basis of attempts at its enhancement holds promise for the assessment and promotion of learning readiness.

***Emotional Functioning***. The topic of emotional self-management or "emotional intelligence" (EI) has drawn much attention among behavioral scientists during the past decade. Salovey and Mayer (1989) introduced the concept with their article *Emotional Intelligence*, in the journal *Imagination, Cognition and Personality*, and Goleman (1995) popularized it in his trade book *Emotional Intelligence*. According to Salovey and Mayer, EI consists in the main of being in touch with one's emotions, being able to sort them out, and being able to regulate them.

| | Emotional Engagement | | |
|---|---|---|---|
| **Self-Regulation** | Being in touch with one's moods and emotions | Sorting out one's moods and emotions | Managing one's moods and emotions |
| Motivation | | | |
| Goal Setting | | | |
| Strategy Usage | | | |
| Self-Evaluation | | | |

**Figure 3.4. Self-Regulation Model of Emotional Intelligence.** From Martinez-Pons (1998).

Martinez-Pons (1999–2000) developed a model of emotional intelligence, appearing in Figure 3.4, combining these components of EI with the self-regulatory process of motivation, goal setting, strategy usage, and self-valuation (self-monitoring and strategy adjustment). The *Self-Regulation Scale of Emotional Intelligence (SRSEI)*, based on this model, appears in Appendix D.

*Emotional Self-Regulation and Academic Performance among College Students.* In the research with graduate students noted earlier, this writer examined the relation of emotional intelligence as the self-regulatory process appearing in Figure 3.4 with academic self-regulation (ASR). As shown in Figure 3.2, a correlation emerged between the two variables ($r = .51$, $p < .05$). It is worth noting that, also as shown in Figure 3.2, emotional self-regulation predicted mental efficiency ($r = .45$, $p < .05$, decreasing to a direct effect of .32 when the intervening effect of academic self-regulation was controlled statistically. These findings suggest that emotional stability is a necessary condition for the psychological processes involved in mental information processing and academic self-regulation and mental efficiency—rendering assessment of emotional self-regulation an important aspect of the diagnosis of the learning readiness of college students.

Thus, mental efficiency and emotional self-regulation are important psychological factors underlying the degree to which students can benefit from the learning experience in the college setting. For this reason, the instructor with information about his or her students' mental efficiency and emotional self-regulation is in a better position to help his or her students to benefit from the teaching-learning effort than is one lacking this information.

**Management of Multiple Social Roles.** Although, as already noted, scholars have begun examining the relation between self-regulation and academic performance in college students, the approach with adults, examining self-regulatory behavior involving *study strategies*, has been limited in that it has tended to overlook the fact that adults experience a challenge to their academic performance not faced by school-age pupils: multiple adult social roles that the former are called upon to play in the course of everyday life—a condition that raises the question of whether self-regulatory behavior regarding multiple social roles can in its own right impact on the academic success of adult learners.

Based on the work of Martinez-Pons, Rosello and Tempestini (1995) on multiple role demands and psychological functioning in adults, Shanley, Martinez-Pons, and Rubal-Lopez (1999) entertained the possibility that difficulty in coping with *multiple role conflict* negatively impacts on academic success among adult learners. They examined the relations that exist between self-regulation of multiple social roles, study skills, and performance on tests of general academic attainment. First, through structured interviews, they identified eight strategies as helpful to successful students in their management of multiple social responsibilities:

1. Prioritizing roles according to their level of importance
2. Prioritizing roles so as to attend to them in their order of urgency
3. Prioritizing roles so as to attend to them in their order of difficulty
4. Developing effective personal skills for enacting each role
5. Having hobbies to help distract one's mind from one's responsibilities
6. Using support groups to help in coping with these responsibilities, as opposed to relying completely on one's own resources
7. Setting time aside for relaxation
8. Using social resources to help in meeting responsibilities

The researchers then examined the degree to which employment of the eight strategies predicted study skills as measured by the *Learning & Study Strategies Inventory* (Weinstein, 1998) and academic subject mastery as measured by the *Liberal Arts and Science Test (LAST;* New York State Education Department, 1999) with 30 graduate students in a school of education in a large urban university. As shown in Figure 3.5,

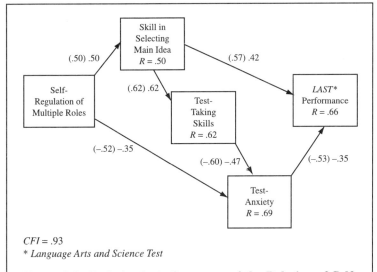

CFI = .93
* Language Arts and Science Test

**Figure 3.5. Path Analysis Outcomes of the Relation of Self-Regulation of Multiple Social Roles and Academic Achievement among Graduate Students.** From Shanley, Martinez-Pons & Rubal-Lopez (1999).

path analysis revealed strong correlations among self-regulation of multiple social roles, study skills, and mastery of academic subjects.

These findings suggest that the personal stability that comes from self-regulatory behavior in the management of multiple social roles positively influences the effectiveness with which adult learners can study, and hence, the quality of their academic performance—and that assessment of self-regulation in the management of multiple social roles is therefore an important aspect of the diagnosis of the learning readiness of college students. It seems clear that the instructor with information about how well his or her students manage their multiple social roles is in a better position to help his or her students to benefit from the teaching-learning effort than is one lacking this information.

Thus, mental efficiency and the degree to which adult students bring self-regulatory skills to bear on such personal processes as emotional soundness, study behavior and the management of multiple social roles forms an important part of their learning readiness. Other elements of learning readiness involve skills for effectively participating in the teaching-learning effort.

## Learning Readiness and the Activities of the College Teaching-Learning Effort

As argued earlier, there are two major sets of activities involved in the highest form of college teaching: the seminar and topic survey, and the instructor-student dialogue and course project (both of these sets of activities are described in Chapter 4). In order to fully participate in the teaching-learning effort, the student must possess skills involving preparation for, participation in, and capitalization on these activities.

**Preparation**. In order to successfully participate in the teaching-learning effort, the student must have a conceptual frame of reference from which to operate, and there are two major sets of tasks that the student must be able perform in developing this mental framework. First, he or she must be able to review works in the literature addressing the topic at hand—an activity through which he or she can identify issues, if any, surrounding the topic at hand, as well as work that may have been conducted to address these issues.[1] Relative to this task, the student must be able to interpret and evaluate this material, and he or she must be able to integrate the material into his or her conceptual framework for thinking about the topic. The second set of tasks the student must be able to perform in preparation for the teaching-learning effort involves the conduct, analysis and interpretation of personal observations of processes in his or her surroundings with relevance to the topic.

Thus, to effectively prepare to participate in the teaching-learning effort, the student must have a conceptual frame of reference from which he or she can approach the endeavor. The skill for initiating this conceptual framework and for integrating into it material gleaned from the literature and personal observations determines the degree to which the student can benefit from the teaching-learning experience, and it thus constitutes a key target in the diagnosis of his or her learning readiness.

**Participation**. Since the seminar and instructor-student dialogue that form the highest form of college instruction are largely exercises in communication, the student must possess the communication skills necessary to effectively participate in these two sets of activities. Such

---

[1] Familiarity with the Internet for this purpose is essential to keep abreast of developments in any modern field of endeavor. For the student learning about the use of this technology to review the literature, Baron (1999) provides an extensive guide to sites with data bases containing references to publications of the past 20 or 30 years in virtually any field.

skills include the ability to clearly describe some object, process, or psychological state to others, or to persuade others relative to a position that the student holds on some issue. Effective communication also requires the disposition and ability to receive, accurately interpret, and constructively respond to messages conveyed to him or her by others. Assessment of these communication skills and dispositions forms an important part of the diagnosis of a student's learning readiness.

**Capitalization**. In the final analysis, there are two things a student must be able to do in order to capitalize on his or her participation in the college teaching-learning effort. He or she must be able to integrate what he or she has learned into his or her topical frame of reference, and he or she must be able to transfer what he or she has gained to situations different from that in which learning has occurred.

***Integration of Learned Material***. To capitalize on the teaching-learning effort, the student must be able to integrate what hc or she has learned into his or her conceptual framework for thinking about the topic at hand. Ways in which he or she can do this is to use the mastered material to expand his or her conceptual framework; to eliminate or modify aspects of it; or to re-organize the framework's structure. Assessment of the ability to integrate material into his or her conceptual framework forms an important part of the diagnosis of a student's learning readiness.

***Transfer of Learned Material***. In addition to the integration of learned material into his or her conceptual framework, the student must be able to transfer whatever knowledge, skill, or disposition he or she has gained from the learning experience to situations different from that in which he or she has attained it. This last requirement is important because, in the words of Davis (1983),

> One of the central purposes of formal education is to teach knowledge, skills and values of future benefit to the learners and to society. [Academic] . . . learning is intended to **transfer** to the world. (p. 207)

It was earlier noted that college instruction is ultimately meant to enable the student to apply what he or she has learned to aspects of the management of his or her life, to the performance of aspects of his or her work, and to aspects of his or her participation in the societal decision-making process. *Transfer* refers to application of mastered material to contexts other than that in which the material has been learned, and therefore, assessment of the ability to transfer gains to novel situations forms an important part of the diagnosis of a student's learning readiness.

It should now be noted that differences between contexts and between tasks can occur at increasing levels of complexity, and that the degree to which the student can transfer mastered material from the learning setting to other settings will likely depend on his or her ability to deal with the complexity level at hand. In fact, individuals differ in their ability to cope with contextual factors, and it is possible for some students to experience more success than others in utilizing learned material to adjust to novel conditions. After reviewing the research literature on transfer, Ceci and Roazzi (1998) concluded, ". . . findings show that thinking skills developed in one context often do not transfer to other contexts, so that cognitive abilities learned in one specific context may well have little impact on performance in connected areas." (p. 84).

On the basis of their review of the literature, Pressley and McCormick (1995) summarized reasons for the failure of learners to transfer acquired material to new situations as follows:

1.  Although they may be able to transfer if given hints on how to do so, students may simply not recognize that knowledge gained in one context can be used in a different context.
2.  At times, the student may realize that the knowledge gained is applicable to a new situation, but, confusing relevant and irrelevant information retained in memory, may use a jumbled strategy that proves ineffective.
3.  The student may not enjoy carrying out the strategy or may not think that the benefits to be derived from the transfer are worth the effort.

Martinez-Pons (2000) argued that problems with the notion of transfer may involve the fact that the phenomenon has been conceptualized as something that either is or is not successfully relocated from one setting to another, instead of as *part of a process* through which one tests the usefulness of combinations of previously acquired items of information or behavioral patterns as one attempts to adapt to new situations. In the author's view, the primary focus regarding transfer should not be the amenability to generalization of a particular item of information or the transfer potential presented by a given expository technique, but the learner's adaptive behavior as he or she attempts to function in novel situations—partly by using combinations of previously and newly acquired information or skills.

In this stance, successful adaptation to new situations is primarily dependent on the self-regulatory skills the person brings to the task. In this view, the dynamics of adaptation, including application, have to do with a process of self-regulation through which a person enacts the following activities. He or she:

1. Perceives a state of affairs requiring some sort of adaptive behavior on his or her part.
2. Analyzes the situation in however much detail he or she deems necessary in order to determine how much of what he or she has in his or her cognitive, affective, or psychomotor repertories that he or she can bring to bear on the situation at hand (area *a* in Figure 3.6), and how much the situation requires new learning on his or her part in order for the adaptive effort to succeed (area *b* in Figure 3.6).

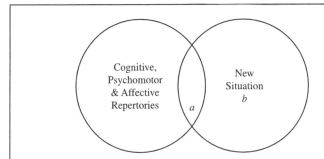

**Figure 3.6. Relation Between an Individual's Psychological Repertory and a Novel Situation.** From Martinez-Pons (2000a). Area *a* depicts elements of a person's psychological repertory applicable to a new situation and Area *b* depicts aspects of the situation requiring new learning for adaptation to take place.

3. Selects and combines elements of previously and newly acquired sets of information or behavioral patterns that he or she estimates will best serve the adaptive effort.
4. Uses the information or enacts the behavioral sets identified in Step 3.
5. Self-monitors to ascertain the degree to which the activities of Step 4 promote the success of the adaptive effort.

6. Modifies the effort as necessary to better accomplish the adaptive goal. He or she performs this task through modification of the existing behavioral sets, inclusion of newly learned sets, or both.

In contrast to previous views of transfer entertaining single, pass-fail attempts to apply individual, intact items of information to novel situations, the present stance recognizes the central role in the process of adaptation played by the self-regulatory processes of strategy planning, strategy usage, self-monitoring and behavioral adjustment.

To test the view of transfer as part of an adaptive process, the researcher administered the *Self-Regulated Transfer Scale (SRTS)*, appearing in Appendix E, to 85 undergraduate and graduate students in a school of education in a large urban university, and to 222 7th- and 8th-grade pupils in a public school in a large urban setting. He also administered the *Five-Component Scale of Academic Self-Regulation* (*FCSSR*; Martinez-Pons, 1999a), a scale of academic self-regulatory behavior addressing academic *motivation, goal-setting, strategy usage, self-monitoring* and *strategy adjustment*. The *FCSSR* appears in Appendix E.

For both the university and middle-school samples, factor analysis outcomes (see Appendix A for a discussion of factor analysis) disclosed two distinct, related factors, with *SRTS* scores loading exclusively on one factor and the *FCSSR* score loading exclusively on the other. For the university sample, the correlation between the factors was $\phi = .62$, and for the middle-school sample it was $\phi = .53$.

For the middle-school sample, path analysis outcomes (see Appendix A for a discussion of path analysis), shown in Figure 3.7, disclosed that while academic self-regulation is related to academic achievement ($r = .32$, $p < .05$), the effect proved to be entirely through mediation of self-regulated transfer behavior ($\beta = 0$). These findings showed that, although general academic self-regulation is an important condition for academic achievement, it is self-regulatory transfer-adaptive behavior which directly influences academic attainment.

Thus, a student's ability to adjust to novel circumstances by combining previously and newly learned material is an important component of a student's learning readiness, and for this reason it forms an important part of the diagnostic facet of the pre-engagement phase of instruction.

In summary, learning readiness consists of the efficiency with which a student can mentally process information, and the degree to which he or she can self-regulate relative to his or her psychological functioning, relative to the management of multiple social role manage-

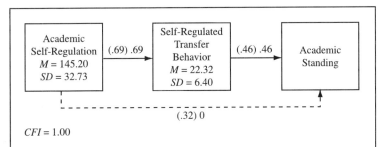

**Figure 3.7. Path Analysis Outcomes for Middle-School Sample.** The broken-lined linkage between academic self-regulation and academic performance is used to show that although the zero-order correlation between these two variables was $r = .32$, $p < .05$, the effect proved to be entirely through mediation of self-regulated transfer behavior.

ment, and relative to participation in the teaching-learning effort. The instructor with information about these aspects of his or her students' functioning is in a better position to help them to benefit from the teaching-learning effort than is one lacking this information.

Appendix G displays a questionnaire the student can use to self-evaluate his or her readiness level regarding preparation for, participation in, and capitalization on the teaching-learning effort; Appendix H displays a questionnaire for the instructor's own assessment of the student's readiness level in this regard; and Figure 3.8 displays an inventory form the instructor can use to record the estimated learning readiness of the student in each area discussed above as well as the estimated level of effort it would require to remedy any deficiencies found.

The instructor can use information he or she generates through the assessment of a student's readiness to participate in the teaching-learning effort a) to decide on the self-regulatory level the student brings to the task; and b), in the case of a student with deficits in these areas, to estimate the amount of effort it would take to remedy the condition. In the case in which the amount of effort would exceed that which the instructor feels he or she can exert, he or she can refer the student to others with the resources necessary to remedy the problem.

The preceding pages discussed diagnostic activities relative to student learning-readiness level. The following pages discuss diagnostic activities relative to the instructor's own readiness to undertake the teaching-learning effort.

| AREA | Self-regulatory level | | | | | Remediation Effort Needed | | | | |
|---|---|---|---|---|---|---|---|---|---|---|
| | *Low* 1 | 2 | 3 | 4 | *High* 5 | *Low* 1 | 2 | 3 | 4 | *High* 5 |
| | M | G | SU | SM | SA | M | G | SU | SM | SA |
| Locating, reviewing, evaluating, and conceptually integrating scholarly material | | | | | | | | | | |
| Conducting, interpreting, and conceptually integrating controlled observations | | | | | | | | | | |
| Recalling, interpreting, and conceptually integrating personal experiences | | | | | | | | | | |
| Integrating information gathered from various sources to prepare for a class discussion | | | | | | | | | | |
| Clearly expressing a position on some issue | | | | | | | | | | |
| Arguing a point with emotional aplomb | | | | | | | | | | |
| Tactfully expressing an opinion | | | | | | | | | | |
| Understanding what others say | | | | | | | | | | |
| Assessing the validity of others' statements | | | | | | | | | | |
| Working in a group to achieve some end | | | | | | | | | | |
| Integrating learned material into a personal world view | | | | | | | | | | |
| Applying learned material in contexts outside the learning setting | | | | | | | | | | |
| Mental efficiency | | | | | | | | | | |
| Emotional Functioning Managing multiple social roles | | | | | | | | | | |

**Figure 3.8.   Student Learning Readiness Inventory.** M = Motivation, G = Goal setting, SU = Strategy Use, SM = Self-monitoring, SA = Strategy Adjustment.

## Information about the Instructor's Readiness to Undertake the Instructional Effort

Crow and Crow (1954) reported the results of a survey in which college students were asked to state what they felt constitutes instructor efficacy. The top ten attributes that emerged making up instructor efficacy, which seem as pertinent today as they did nearly half a century ago, can be broken down into three areas of performance: pedagogical expertise, knowledge of the content area at hand, and commitment to teaching.

**Pedagogical Expertise**
1. Systematic organization of subject matter
2. Speaking ability
3. Ability to explain clearly
4. Ability to encourage thought
5. Fairness in grading tests
6. Tolerance toward student disagreement

**Knowledge of the Content Area at Hand**
7. Expert knowledge of subject

**Commitment to Teaching**
8. Sympathetic attitude toward students
9. Enthusiastic attitude toward subject
10. Pleasing personality

In addition to the attributes reported by Crow and Crow (1954), instructor commitment can be generally defined as a desire to remain in the field of education; and, more specifically, as a measure of the time and effort the instructor is typically willing to devote to his or her craft, and of the time and effort he or she is willing to devote to overcome difficulties encountered in the course of teaching. Appendix I shows a self-report questionnaire the instructor can use to gauge his or her readiness to undertake the teaching-learning effort.

Chapter 3 has described that facet of the pre-engagement phase of instruction through which the educator gathers information about the needs to be addressed through instruction and about his or her own and his or her students' readiness to undertake the teaching-learning effort. Chapter 4 discusses that facet of the pre-engagement phase of instruction through which the educator plans the activities of instruction.

# Chapter 4

---

# Planning

## INTRODUCTION

Chapter 3 described the generation of information concerning a) that which the instructional effort is to involve, b) the readiness level of students to participate in the teaching-learning effort, and c) the instructor's own preparation to undertake the instructional endeavor. Chapter 4 describes ways in which the instructor can use this information in his or her planning of the instructional effort.

In the planning facet of college instruction, the educator develops instructional objectives on the basis of information he or she has gathered through needs-assessment activities, and he or she develops assessment methodology to determine the degree to which students attain the instructional objectives. In addition, in this facet of college instruction the educator develops the engagement procedures through which he or she will aid his or her students in their pursuit of the instructional objectives. Finally, at this point the educator develops any remediation procedures indicated by diagnostic findings.

## DEVELOPMENT OF INSTRUCTIONAL OBJECTIVES

The term "instructional objectives" refers to a set of statements regarding that which instruction is to enable students to do. Instructional objectives are developed for each area of concern identified through the needs-assessment effort described in Chapter 3.

A central concept in modern theorization about instructional objectives is that of the *domain*. Domains are general areas of human behavior around which instruction is planned and executed. The areas of learning that have been traditionally addressed in the formulation of instructional objectives date back to Aristotle, who held that all human behavior takes affective, cognitive, or psychomotor form.

There exist a number of taxonomies of instructional objectives developed on the basis of Aristotle's tripartite conceptualization of human behavior. Some of the more widely known are that of Bloom, Englehart, Furst, Hill and Krathwohl (1956) for objectives for the cognitive domain; that of Krathwohl, Bloom and Masia (1964) for objectives for the affective domain and those of Simpson (1972) and Kibler, Barker and Miles (1970) for objectives for the psychomotor domain. The elements of each of these taxonomies are arranged in a hierarchical order ranging between simplest to most complex, with mastery at one level said to be necessary for mastery at higher levels to occur. For example, the components of the cognitive taxonomy of Bloom et al. are organized in six ascending levels of complexity: knowledge, comprehension, application, analysis, synthesis, and evaluation. For this taxonomy, beyond knowledge, mastery at each level is said to depend on mastery at the level immediately below it.

Some reservations have been expressed concerning early taxonomies of instructional objectives. First, arguing that the view of cognitive, affective and psychomotor domains as separate entities is too fragmentary to provide a realistic framework for instructional planning, Gagné (1964) combined cognitive, affective and psychomotor learning outcomes into one single taxonomy. His conceptual framework consists of *verbal information* (facts, processes, etc.), *intellectual skills* (discrimination, classification, rule application), *cognitive strategies* (ways of learning and remembering new things), *attitudes* (values, fears, self-concept), and *motor skills* (writing, operating computers and using tools).

In addition to concerns involving fragmentation into separate, independent domains, some scholars have expressed reservations regarding the level of direct observability stipulated by the authors of some early taxonomies. While Mager (1962) conceptualized instructional objectives in strictly observable terms, Gronlund (1978) argued that, particularly when the objectives involve mastery of such directly un-observable processes as concepts and values, it is necessary to refer to these abstract entities as well as to their observed manifestations when they are in fact involved in the goals of instruction. Gagné (1964) adhered to this view in his inclusion of attitudes, which are unobservable psychological processes, in his own formulation of instructional objectives.

A third concern voiced regarding existing taxonomies of instructional objectives involves the rationale for their hypothesized hierarchical structures. For example, Furst (1981) questioned the hier-archical order stipulated among the components of Bloom's taxonomy for the cognitive domain, arguing that to say that knowledge occurs *before* comprehension is to overlook the fact that often the acquisition of new knowledge is impossible without the comprehension of prior knowledge—or without comprehension of the information's relevance for the learner. In fact, a related, fourth, reservation concerning existing taxonomies of instructional objectives concerns the empirical validity of their hypothesized internal order. To this writer's knowledge, only Bloom's taxonomy has received any extensive empirical testing (see Kropp and Stoker, 1966; Madaus, Woods and Nuttall, 1973; Seddon, 1978; Miller, Snowman and O'Hara, 1979; Martinez-Pons, 2001); none of the studies found testing this framework have supported the taxonomy's proposed hierarchical structure.

## A Conceptual Framework of Instructional Objectives

The following conceptual framework of instructional objectives was formulated partly on the basis of modern instructional theory, and partly on the basis of the author's experiences in his own instructional activities. The framework, revolving around the concepts of the affective, cognitive and psychomotor domains, has three distinct features. First, while attending to the unique characteristics of each domain, it also addresses commonalities that exist among them. In terms of this frame-work, displayed in Figure 4.1, the domains of instructional objectives share in common the fact that in each case, the general goals of instruc-tion are the student's acquisition, retention, and utilization of the material addressed through the teaching-learning effort.

The second distinct feature of the model of instructional objectives appearing in Figure 4.1 is that no necessary hierarchy is stipulated among the categories of any of the domains—allowing for the possibility that for a particular instructional effort, some non-

| Domain | Performance Target | | | | | |
|---|---|---|---|---|---|---|
| | | | Utilization | | | |
| | | | Generation of New Material | | Application | |
| | Acquisition | Retention | Internal Restructuring | Combination with Other Material | To the Original Task | To a Novel Task |
| **Affective** *Emotions* | | | | | | |
| *Feelings* | | | | | | |
| *Dispositions* | | | | | | |
| **Cognitive** *Facts* | | | | | | |
| *Concepts* | | | | | | |
| *Algorithms* | | | | | | |
| **Psychomotor** *Operative* | | | | | | |
| *Expressive* | | | | | | |

**Figure 4.1. Conceptual Framework of Institutional Objectives**

hierarchical combination of the elements of a given domain will be necessary for the student to reach the objectives of instruction; or that while a specific sequence among the elements may be involved among the elements in one case, a different sequence may be involved in another.

The third distinct feature of the model appearing in Figure 4.1 involves the fixed functional relations it specifies: while it does not postulate a restricted hierarchical order among the domains' areas, the model does stipulate a fixed functional relation, described below, among the acquisition, retention and utilization elements of the framework. The following discussion of the present conceptualization of instructional objectives follows the model appearing in Figure 4.1.

### The Domains of Instructional Objectives

The first major area in Figure 4.1, *Domain*, refers to the affective, cognitive, and psychomotor spheres of human behavior.

## The Affective Domain

When planning instruction involving the affective domain, the educator typically asks himself or herself, "Do I want to address ways in which students can regulate their emotions, to elicit in students feelings relative to some topic, or to engender in students a disposition to behave in some way? Emotions, feelings, and dispositions are major affective processes addressed by instructional objectives for the affective domain.

**Emotions.** An emotion is a response to a condition perceived in either positive or negative terms relative to a person's well-being or value system—a response involving the potential for some form of behavior (or behavioral restraint) relative to the source of the perception. Four emotions are of particular interest regarding the modern adult: anxiety (anticipation of a threatening condition resulting in intense apprehension, uncertainty, and fear, often intense enough to interfere with physical and psychological functioning); depression (a state of extreme sadness, dejection, and hopelessness, often accompanied by insomnia, withdrawal, inability to concentrate and reduction in physiological vigor); anger (a strong feeling of displeasure or hostility often accompanied by an urge to attack the source of the emotion); and elation (a state of happiness, often accompanied by expressions of joy and heightened constructive activity).

Instructional objectives addressing emotions can be mapped on the basis of the *Self-Regulation Model of Emotional Intelligence (SRMEI)* proposed by Martinez-Pons (1999–2000), described in Chapter 3, and shown in Figure 4.2.

| Self-Regulation | Emotional Engagment | | |
|---|---|---|---|
| | Being in touch with one's moods and emotions | Sorting out one's moods and emotions | Managing one's moods and emotions |
| Motivation | a | b | c |
| Goal Setting | d | e | f |
| Strategy Usage | g | h | i |
| Self-Evaluation | j | k | l |

**Figure 4.2. Self-Regulation Model of Emotional Intelligence.** From Martinez-Pons (1998).

As noted by the author,

> In the case in which a person is experiencing emotional difficulties, it may be important to pinpoint the self-regulatory EI component (i.e., that component represented by a given cell of the SRMEI) in which the problem occurs, and to then concentrate intervention efforts in this area. This approach would prevent the form of wasted effort involved when the problem lies in, say, low *motivation* to manage one's emotions (*Cell c*) and the attempt is directed solely at, say, training in *strategy skills* for managing one's emotions (*Cell i*). (p. 342)

**Feelings**. A feeling is a sensation such as "a feeling of warmth" or "a feeling of excitement", or ". . . feelings of hope and joy; a feeling of inferiority; religious feeling" (*American Heritage Dictionary*; Houghton Mifflin Company, 2000). Although associated with emotions, feelings can occur independently of such emotional processes as interpretation of the situation at hand as friendly or hostile, or a drive to take some sort of action relative to the object of the emotion. An example of a feeling as an instructional objective involves students developing a feeling of pride in their academic involvement.

**Dispositions**. A disposition is a conditioned tendency to behave in a given way relative to some object (e.g., to approach, avoid, support, oppose, seek out, defend, attack, accept, or reject the thing of interest). Examples of dispositions are a determination to vote in elections for public office, a tendency to avoid interacting with persons of a particular group, a propensity to reject any statement made by a member of an opposing political party—and a disposition to study until the work is completed.

Thus, emotions, feelings, and dispositions are major affective processes addressed by instructional objectives for the affective domain.

## The Cognitive Domain

When planning instruction involving the cognitive domain, the educator typically asks himself or herself, "Do I want to teach a set of facts, a set of concepts, or a set of algorithms—or some combination of the three?" Facts, concepts or principles, and algorithms for conducting mental tasks are major topics addressed by instructional objectives for the cognitive domain.

**Facts**. A fact is an item of information considered objectively real (for example, the distance between New York and Paris). According to the *American Heritage Dictionary* (Houghton Mifflin Company, 2000), while some theorists differentiate between *true facts* and *real facts*, other workers hold that facts cannot be other than true. This author's view is that a fact need only be a piece of information *purported* to be real, the proposition always subject to corroboration.

**Concepts.** A concept is the mental summary of an attention-eliciting pattern of attributes or processes that seem to occur together, as a unit. An example of a concept is that of *intelligence* described in Chapter 3, involving the speed with which people *assimilate* new information, the effectiveness with which they *remember* the information, and the extent to which they can *utilize* the information. This author has argued that these processes are so closely related in mental information processing that a conceptual summary holding them as a mental unit and termed *intelligence* is justified (Martinez-Pons, 1997). Concepts can be arranged in models that depict relations occurring among them.

**Algorithms.** An algorithm is a series of steps for accomplishing some task, usually of a mental nature. Pedagogically, an algorithm becomes particularly useful when it includes a description of the mental faculty involved at each step in the process as well as the rules for executing the step. An example of an algorithm is that of the description of the "scientific method", usually described as a process involving five steps (Martinez-Pons, 1996): problem identification and description, dependent on the psychological process of *curiosity* and guided by the rule that the problem at hand must be described in observable terms; the search for clues regarding the factors underlying the problem, relying on the mental process of *analysis*, and guided by the rule that the search must be conducted within the situation in which the problem occurs; development of hypotheses as tentative solutions to the problem, relying on the psychological process of *creativity*, and guided by the rule that more than one hypothesis should be developed to raise the likelihood of identifying the actual factor or factors underlying the problem; testing of the hypotheses, relying on the mental process of *syllogistic reasoning* and guided by the rule that the effort must be to *disprove* rather than prove as many of the hypotheses as possible; and deciding on the degree to which the problem has been solved, relying on the mental process of *synthesis*, or integration of supported hypotheses into one cohesive whole to tell the complete story—and guided by the rule that, typically, an effort must be made to identify *factors and their interactions contributory to the problem* rather than to the identity of one factor as sole cause of the problem.

Thus, facts, concepts, and algorithms for conducting mental tasks are major topics addressed by instructional objectives for the cognitive domain.

## The Psychomotor Domain

When planning instruction involving the psychomotor domain, the educator typically asks himself or herself, "Do I want to teach students how to elicit or prevent a change in some object or process, or how to perform some act of communication?" In either case, goal-oriented, co-ordinated, physical activity is the process addressed by instructional objectives for the psychomotor domain.

While the psychomotor domain contains an element of physical movement, it also involves the important self-regulatory mental components of goal setting and self-monitoring to gauge the success of goal-seeking physical activity. It is this interplay of motor action with self-monitoring that has led theorists to conceptualize the psychomotor domain as a unitary process involving physical and self-regulatory components. Two major behavioral forms are stipulated in the present conceptualization of the psychomotor domain of instructional objectives: operative and expressive.

**Operative Psychomotor Behavior**. Operative psychomotor behavior involves physical activity whose purpose is the attainment or maintenance of some process or personal state. *Self-oriented* operative psychomotor behavior is intended to bring about or maintain some personal skill (for example, practicing to correctly execute a dance step or a swim stroke) or state (for example, performing a weight lifting exercise to develop or maintain muscle strength, performing a breathing exercise to relax); and *object-oriented* operative psychomotor behavior involves physical activity intended to bring about or maintain some state or process in an external object or situation (for example, using a drill to bore a hole through a wood panel, making continual minute corrective adjustments with a car's steering wheel to keep the car traveling in a straight line).

**Expressive Psychomotor Behavior**. Expressive psychomotor behavior involves physical activity with the purpose of formulating and conveying a message to an audience. It can occur verbally, in the form of an oral or written statement; or non-verbally, in the form of a facial expression, a gesture, or physical activity involving any other form of pantomime.

Thus the affective (emotions, feelings, dispositions), cognitive (facts, concepts, algorithms), and psychomotor (operative, expressive) domains of human behavior are typically addressed in the college teaching-learning effort. While domain forms in addition to those stipulated above and enclosed in parentheses in this summary are possible, those noted here are deemed by this writer to represent major areas of instructional interest for the modern college educator.

It is possible for the instructor to use combinations of the affective, cognitive, and psychomotor domains in any given instructional effort. For example, in teaching a swimming student how to properly execute a butterfly stroke, the instructor may first want to insure the student's disposition to want to learn the procedure (an objective involving the affective domain), and to then insure that the student understands the physiological processes involved in the performance of the stroke (an objective involving the cognitive domain)—following which he or she can proceed to help the student to master the stroke (an objective involving the psychomotor domain).

Having decided on the domain or domains he or she will address through the teaching-learning effort, the instructor can proceed to consider what he or she wants his or her students to be able to do with the material to be taught. This task involves specifying the *performance targets of instruction.*

## The Performance Targets of Instruction

The second major area in Figure 4.1, *Performance Target*, refers to what the educator wants students to be able to do with the material covered in instruction. Three major targets are involved in instruction for any of the three domains of human behavior discussed above: the acquisition, retention, and utilization of the material addressed through the instructional effort.

### Acquisition

The *Acquisition* column in Figure 4.1 involves the learner's reception, interpretation, evaluation, acceptance, and integration of instructional material into his or her conceptual framework for addressing the topic. The student manifests his or her attainment of this objective by enacting for the first time the behavior of interest according to some set of criteria following instruction.

### Retention

The *Retention* column in Figure 4.1 refers to the learner's remembering what he or she has acquired; in addition to memory, retention involves the timely recall of the material when the occasion arises calling for its use. The student manifests attainment of this objective by re-enacting the behavior after a time lapse following acquisition.

## Utilization

The *Utilization* column in Figure 4.1 refers to the things the student does with the material he or she acquires through the teaching-learning effort, beyond enactment of the original behavior. There are two ways in which the student can utilize the material he or she acquires through the instructional effort: he or she can use it to generate new material, or he or she can apply it to complete some task.

**Generation of New Material**. As suggested in Figure 4.1, there are two ways in which the learner can generate new material on the basis of previously mastered material: by restructuring it (e.g., by transforming the equation $R = B N W$ into $B = R / N W$, $N = R / Q W$, or $W = R / B N$); or by combining the material with other material to generate new material (for example, putting together the information that "all men are mortal" with the newly acquired information that "Socrates is a man" to generate the new information that "Socrates is mortal").

**Application of the Material**. In addition to generating new material on the basis of what he or she has learned, the student can apply the material to accomplish some goal. There are two ways in which he or she can utilize the material in this way. First he or she can apply it to the original learning task—for example, after demonstrating at midpoint during a class period that he can solve the problem

$$1/3 + 3/7 = ?$$

the student can solve it again at the end of the class period, showing that he or she has retained mastery of the process. Second, the student can apply the material to a novel task—for example, having demonstrated through the solution of the above problem his or her mastery of the rule for solving problems involving the addition of simple fractions, the student can apply the rule to solve a new problem:

$$2/6 + 5/9 = ?$$

In addition to the application of mastered material across tasks, the student can apply it in the same context in which he or she has acquired it or in a context different from that in which he or she mastered it. Appendix K addresses in some detail combinations of cross-task and cross-context application of mastered instructional material.

Thus, the present framework of instructional objectives addresses the affective, cognitive and psychomotor domains of human behavior—and it stipulates acquisition, retention, and utilization processes as the general targets of instruction common to the three domains. Figure 4.3 displays the relations that exist between instruction and the

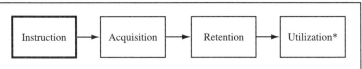

* Generation of new information and application of information

**Figure 4.3. Relations among Instruction and the Student Outcomes of Instructional Objectives.** The heavy-lined box shows instruction as external to but necessary for the student outcomes stipulated in instructional objectives.

three major targets of performance of instructional objectives. The model appearing in this figure assumes that effectiveness of student acquisition of material is dependent at least in part on the effectiveness of instruction; that effectiveness of retention is dependent on the effectiveness of acquisition; and that the effectiveness of application depends on the effectiveness with which the learner retains the material.

### Criteria for Well-Developed Instructional Objectives

Scholars have proposed three criteria for the evaluation of instructional objectives, regardless of the domain involved (Gage and Berliner, 1984). These are *conditions of performance, observability* and *performance criteria.*

### Conditions of Performance

The conditions under which the behavior stipulated in the instructional objective is to take place should be specified. For example, "Given a printed pencil and paper multiple-choice test . . ."

### Observability

The terminal behavior specified in the instructional objective should be stated in action words, since actions can be observed. For example, ". . . the student will place a pencil mark next to the correct answer for each question . . ."

### Performance Criteria

Objectives should specify the criteria that will be used to determine whether the student has met the objective. For example, ". . . for at least 80 percent of the questions."

A fourth criterion, one proposed by this author (Martinez-Pons, 2001), is the *time frame* within which the student should be able to meet the objectives. For example, ". . . within a period of one hour, following a period of instruction lasting no longer than one semester."

## TASK ANALYSIS

Sometimes it is useful to identify performance levels that a student must attain before attempting to reach some set of instructional objectives; Gagné (1964) termed this process *task analysis*.

Two types of task analysis exist: technological and psychological. In its technological form, the approach involves the identification of tasks necessary to achieve some external goal. For example, in building a house, technological task analysis would stipulate that first, the foundation must be laid; that second, the walls must be erected; and that then, the roof can be put in place. In psychological task analysis, the affective, cognitive, or psychomotor subprocesses are identified that are prerequisites for the student's attainment of the instructional objectives at hand. Often, these subprocesses can be arranged in a certain sequence, with that which the learner has already mastered termed his or her *entry level* for the purpose of instructional planning. The following example of a psychological task analysis is taken from Martinez-Pons (2001):

> . . . assume that the terminal behavior stipulated in an instructional objective is being able to divide whole numbers. A task analysis of this objective might take the following form:
>
> 1. Knowledge of numbers
> 2. Addition skills
> 3. Subtraction skills

    4.   Multiplication skills
    5.   **Division skills**

Item 5, appearing in bold face, refers to the terminal behavior stipulated in the instructional objectives, and items 1 to 4 refer to the skills necessary to reach the terminal behavior. To ensure that the student reaches the terminal behavior in item 5, the instructor would first ensure that the student can function at level 4, level 3, and so on. (p. 106)

In education, early versions of task analysis tended to center exclusively on the instructor's decomposition of instructional objectives into subprocesses. While this approach has seemed to work well at the primary and secondary school levels for lower-level thinking skills, for the higher-level thinking skills that typically form the objectives of college instruction, the early approach has come to be seen as wanting. According to Derry and Lesgold (1998),

Many educators now believe that beyond intellectual skills and verbal knowledge, higher order thinking capabilities are the most important goals for schooling. As traditional instructional design theory does not address these types of learning outcome, it is not capable of addressing the challenges associated with the winds of corporate and educational reform that are sweeping our country today. (p. 788)

To address this issue, Derry and Lesgold (1998) developed a *process of successive approximation* that enables the instructor to overcome the limitations of early task-analysis forms. This method includes the following steps:

    1.   Observing the way in which an expert enacts the behavior in question and questioning him or her regarding behavioral details
    2.   Constructing a tentative representation of the expert's knowledge
    3.   Formulating a sequential algorithm that can be enacted by the task analyst and critiqued by the expert
    4.   Repeating the process with the task analyst taking the place of the expert, and the student taking the place previously taken by the task analyst.

According to Derry and Lesgold (1998), this method involves

Some give and take, dialectic, between the task analyst and the expert.

> Further . . . knowledge acquisition by the student must also involve this negotiation of meaning. Consequently, it is critically important that the outcome of knowledge engineering be not only the meaning finally understood by the task analyst but also a process for negotiating meaning with the student that can lead to the student's having a functionally similar body of knowledge after learning. (p. 802)

For college instruction at its highest level, this approach to task analysis becomes particularly important in remediation, when it becomes necessary to enable students to acquire prerequisite skills for participating in the teaching-learning effort. The instructor-student interactive feature of modern task analysis is especially relevant given Knowles' (1970) work stipulating the adult learner as an active participant in the planning of instructional activities.

Once the instructor has formulated the objectives of instruction and worked out any necessary task analysis for the instructional objectives, he or she can proceed to identify or develop the assessment methodology he or she will use to determine the success of the instructional effort.

## ASSESSMENT

Once the instructor has completed his or her teaching effort, he or she must have some way of determining whether his or her attempt has been successful in enabling his or her students to attain the instructional objectives at hand. For college instruction, assessment is used to, among other things, determine a student's entry level relative to the topic at hand as well as the student's performance level following instruction.

### Assessment Forms

There are many types of assessment instruments—so many, in fact, that some authors have sought some way to classify them to facilitate their discussion. Fox's (1969) taxonomy will be used in the following discussion of assessment. This taxonomy consists of three categories into which assessment instruments can be placed: *questioning tools*, *observation tools*, and *measurement tools*. On the basis of Fox's taxonomy, Figure 4.4, adapted from Martinez-Pons (1996, 2001), summarizes the forms of assessment instruments available to the educator, their subtypes, the way in which they are used, and their typical assessment targets.

| Instrument Attributes | Instrument Type | | |
|---|---|---|---|
| | **Questioning** | **Observation** | **Measurement** |
| Subtypes | Interviews Questionnaires Checklists Critical incident reports | Systematic Random | Tests Projectives Inventories Sociograms Scaling techniques |
| Approach | Information provided by an informant is usually taken as given | Information obtained directly, without the aid of an informant, is used as the data | Information provided by an informant or through direct observation is interpreted according to some standard |
| Typical Assessment Target | Opinions Demographics Social processes Attitudes Motivation | Social processes Individual behavior Grounded theory research | Intelligence Academic achievement Personality Depression |

**Figure 4.4. Types of Assessment Instruments and Their Use.**
From Martinez-Pons (1996).

## Questioning Tools

The instructor employs questioning tools when he or she is interested in using the obtained information he or she obtains through the assessment effort at face value, without imputing into it any meaning beyond the original data. With this type of assessment tool, respondents provide their answers in their own words or select their responses from a list of alternatives. For example, a questionnaire item can ask, "On a scale ranging between 1 ("*Completely disagree*") and 7 ("*Completely agree*"), what is your position regarding the statement that intelligence tests should be abolished?" The respondent's answer is taken at face value, with no interpretation of what it suggests regarding, say, his or her personality. Forms of questioning tools are *individual* and *focus group interview schedules*; *questionnaires* and *checklists*; and *critical incident queries*, in which the respondent is asked to describe or judge a person's behavior under given circumstances.

## Observation Tools

The instructor uses observation tools when he or she is interested in recording the frequency, duration, or intensity of behavior.

## Measurement Tools

The instructor interprets the data he or she gathers through the use of measurement tools on the basis of some frame of reference or standard. Such concerns as achievement level, intelligence level, self-concept quality, personality type, and depression level are addressed through the use of measurement tools.

*Projective techniques* are measurement tools that use ambiguous cues, responses to which the educator can use to infer something about the subject's personality; *inventories* are measurement tools the educator can use for indications of whether or not any set of attributes are true of the respondent; *sociometric* techniques are measurement tools the educator can use to ascertain a group's overall cohesiveness on the basis of which group members indicate those individuals with whose sociometric techniques they would want to interact in various ways; and *scaling* techniques are measurement tools the educator can use to assess judgments of magnitude regarding stimuli.

Of particular interest to the college instructor is that form of measuring instrument termed the *test*. Because this form of assessment is predominant in college instruction, it will be addressed in some detail in the following paragraphs.

Tests are measurement tools the educator uses to categorize the information generated in some way according to stated criteria. For example, a score of 50 on a mathematics test would be interpreted as a failing grade if the passing criterion has been set at 80; and a certain score profile on a personality test might be interpreted as indicative of a compulsive personality according to some frame of reference for interpreting the profile.

Three features of tests are of special interest to the college instructor: their *format*, their *reference*, and their *source*. Concerning the first feature, a test can take a *forced-choice* format such as a multiple-choice exam, or an *open-ended* format such as an essay exam. Concerning the second feature, a test can be *criterion-referenced* or *norm-referenced*. Criterion-referenced tests are used to assess the degree to which specific instructional objectives have been met, and norm-referenced tests are used to compare students' performance with that of others. Concerning the third feature, a test can be generated by the instructor or it can be generated by an outside party such as a publisher of assessment instruments.

Combinations of the format, reference, and source features produces eight different kinds of test available to the college instructor. Figure 4.5 shows the combinations possible among the format, reference

| Format | Reference | Source | |
|---|---|---|---|
| | | Instructor | External |
| Forced-Choice | Criterion | 1 | 2 |
| | Norm | 3 | 4 |
| Open-Ended | Criterion | 5 | 6 |
| | Norm | 7 | 8 |

**Figure 4.5.  Forms of Tests by Format, Reference and Source**

and source categories of assessment instruments. The cell values in this table show the level of appropriateness of each test type for the purpose of criterion-referenced testing. Tests corresponding to cells 1 and 5 (criterion-referenced, instructor-generated tests), followed by tests corresponding to cells 2 and 6 (criterion-referenced, externally-generated tests), are more likely to "map on" to the criteria of the objectives of some instructional effort than are tests with other cell numbers.

The cell values in Figure 4.5 also show the level of appropriateness of each test type for the purpose of norm-referenced testing. Tests corresponding to cells 4 and 8 (norm-referenced, externally produced tests), followed by tests corresponding to cells 3 and 7 (norm-referenced, instructor-generated tests) are more relevant to the assessment of student performance *by reference to a population* than are tests corresponding to other cell numbers.

Assessment instruments and procedures in addition to those considered above exist, falling under the rubric of *authentic assessment*. A certain amount of controversy surrounds these approaches to assessment; Martinez-Pons (2001) describes these forms of assessment and discusses the controversy that attends them at present.

## Assessment Instrument Development

Martinez-Pons (1996) proposed the following steps in the development of any assessment instrument:

1. Determine the skill, behavior or value the student is to manifest following Instruction.
2. Determine the instrument type to use.
3. Generate the instrument's items.
4. Design the instrument's layout.
5. Develop an initial draft of the instrument.
6. Develop the administration procedures.
7. Develop the scoring and interpretation protocols.
8. Conduct pilot testing and make instrumental modifications as necessary.
9. Validate the instrument. (See below for a discussion of validity).
10. When the instrument is to be used as a norm-referenced tool, develop the instrument's norms.

Callahan, Clark and Kellough (1998), Childs (1989) and Williams (1991) have written clear, easy to follow texts on the construction of teacher-produced tests.

## Properties of Acceptable Assessment Instruments

An assessment instrument must possess two principal properties in order to be considered appropriate for use in education: It must be valid and it must be reliable.

### Validity

Validity involves the degree to which an assessment instrument addresses its subject matter. In the past, measurement theorists differentiated between *face validity*, or the degree to which a lay person can tell whether an instrument's items address what the instrument is said to address; *content validity*, or the degree to which the instrument's items address the theory on which the instrument is based; *criterion validity*, or the degree to which the test agrees with other measures of the same thing; and *construct validity*, or the degree to which the instrument reflects the nature of the construct in question. Modern assessment theorists take a different view of validity. First, they hold that face validity is not validity at all; second, they hold content and criterion validity to be parts of construct validity (Anastasi, 1982). Martinez-Pons, M. (1996) treats these concerns under one comprehensive validity model and describes the manner in which construct validity is determined through the use of modern statistical methodology.

For criterion-referenced assessment, a second major aspect of validity, termed here *objectives-related validity*, involves the degree to which a test addresses performance *in the domain* (*cognitive, affective* or *psychomotor*) and *at the domain area* stipulated in the instructional objectives. In addition, a criterion-referenced test's makeup must be such that it adheres to the conditions of performance stipulated in the objectives of instruction. Finally, to be valid, criterion-referenced test's grading instructions must adhere to the performance standards stipulated in the objectives. Martinez-Pons (1996) describes the statistical methodology used to assess validity.

**Reliability**

Reliability refers to the consistency with which an assessment instrument assesses what it assesses. Such forms of reliability exist as *test-retest reliability*, or the degree to which an instrument assesses its target across time; *interjudge reliability*, or the degree to which different persons agree on their assessment of some behavior or process; and *internal consistency*, or the degree to which all the items in an instrument address the same thing). Martinez-Pons (1996) describes the statistical methodology used to assess assessment instrument reliability, and Appendix A summarizes this methodology.

Additional desired qualities of assessment instruments were proposed by Linn, Baker and Dunbar (1991): *test score interpretation that has consequences for instruction, cultural fairness, transfer and generalizability of scores to achievement more broadly defined than that which the test covers, cognitive complexity at the higher levels of the cognitive domain, content consistent with current knowledge in the area, representation of the different features of the topic at hand, use of problems and tasks meaningful to the examinee, administration efficiency and manageable cost.*

Once the instructor has selected the assessment instruments he or she will use to gauge the success of the instructional undertaking, he or she must consider the manner in which he or she will utilize them to insure the credibility of the information he or she will generate through the assessment effort. This issue involves the matter of research design.

## Research Design in Instructional Assessment

Research design in college instructional assessment involves the manner in which the educator generates information so as to ensure the credibility of assessment findings. There are three *artifacts*, or processes generating misleading assessment findings, for which the instructor must control to insure the credibility of his or her assessment findings: *pre-instruction achievement level, historical effects*, and *test-retest effects*. The following paragraphs discuss the control of these artifacts in the design of instructional assessment.

### Controlling for Pre-Instruction Achievement Level

According to Draves,

> Assessing entering behavior is probably the least recognized and performed step in conducting a course in which a change in behavior is to be measured. Assessing entering behavior is necessary to determine what the person has learned during the course. Testing at the end helps, but certainly does not measure course achievement if entering behavior is not measured. (p. 33)

To illustrate the importance of controlling for pre-instruction achievement level or entering behavior, assume that the objectives of an instructional module stipulate passing a pencil-and-paper multiple-choice test with at least 80 percent accuracy, and all the students in a class perform above this level on a post-test. Whether the instructor can conclude on the basis of this finding that instruction has been successful in enabling the students to reach the objectives depends on how well the students performed before instruction: if pre-test scores disclose that every member of the class performed with or above 85 percent accuracy on a pre-test covering the same information as the post-test, then, unless the purpose of instruction was to *prevent performance loss rather than to improve performance*, the instructor may have to conclude that the students had met the objectives before instruction—and that in fact, instruction had little or nothing to do with post-test performance.

### Controlling for Historical Effects

Historical effects are events that occur during instruction which, while not part of the instructional activities, nevertheless influence post-test performance. One way the college instructor can control for historical effects is through the use of control groups. For example, assume that every student in the class above scored with accuracy significantly below 85 percent on a pre-test and that everyone scored with accuracy significantly above 85 percent on the post-test. Whether the educator can now conclude that instruction has been effective relative to the instructional objectives depends on how the findings compare with those of a control group whose members have not undergone the same instruction. If the members of the control group perform on the pre- and post-tests at the same levels as the members of the instructional group, then the educator may have to conclude that something other than the instruction brought about the post-test outcomes.

Campbell and Stanley (1963) argued that the way to control for the above artifacts is to use a pre-test, post-test design involving experimental and control groups. In this approach, the experimental and control groups receive the pre- and post-tests, but only subjects in the experimental group receive the intervention. This research design appears in Figure 4.6. In this figure, $O$ stands for "observation" or testing, and $X$ stands for "experimental intervention" or instruction. This research plan, termed the *pretest, posttest control group design (PPCGD)*, is one of the more sophisticated of the research schemes available to the college instructor.

| | Pre-Test | Instruction | Post-Test |
|---|---|---|---|
| **Experimental Group:** | $O_1$ | X | $O_2$ |
| **Control group:** | $O_3$ | | $O_4$ |

**Figure 4.6. Pretest, Posttest Control Group Design**

Even if post-test scores of the instruction and control groups are close enough to be indistinguishable, the *PPCGD* enables the educator to conclude that instruction has been effective if test result comparisons yield the following results:

$$O_4 = O_3$$
$$O_2 > O_1$$
$$O_3 > O_1$$

## Controlling for Test-Retest Effects

Finally, when a control group shows the same gains as the instruction group on a post-test, it may be due to the fact that taking a test twice can enable a person to perform better on it the second time. A design used to control for this artifact, using two control groups and two experimental groups and termed the *Solomon pretest, posttest, multiple control group design* (*SPPMCD*), was described by Campbell and Stanley (1969).

When the instructor assigns students to each of the groups in a research effort at random, the design is termed *experimental*, and when he or she does not do so, the design is termed *quasi-experimental*. Thus, the essence of the term *experiment* involves randomization, rather than merely the manipulation of any of the processes at hand.

In most cases, because of the number of groups required by the *PPCGD* and *SPPMCD*, the instructor may find their use impractical. Still, it is important to emphasize that, particularly when randomization is not involved, the credibility of assessment findings depends on the degree to which the research design approximates that of the *PPCGD* or the *SPPMCD*. When randomization is limited, as it is in the typical instructional effort, the most restricted useful design is the one shown in Figure 4.6, using an experimental group and a control group and pre- and post-tests. On the other hand, if the instructor can assign students at random to the two groups, he or she needs only use a post-test, as shown in Figure 4.7, to determine instructional success.

|  | Instruction | Post-Test |
|---|---|---|
| **Experimental Group:** | X | $O_1$ |
| **Control Group:** |  | $O_2$ |

**Figure 4.7. Post-Test Control Group Research Design**

Thus, to insure the credibility of his or her assessment efforts, the instructor must control for pre- and post-test performance, historical, and test-retest effects. Credible research design in testing typically requires the use of pre- and post-tests and control groups. When randomization is possible, the educator may be able to use the post-test only design shown in Figure 4.7.

Once he or she has completed the development of the research design for his or her assessment effort, the instructor can proceed to plan the activities he or she and his or her students will undertake in the instructional effort. This step falls under the heading of *development of the engagement plan*.

## DEVELOPMENT OF THE ENGAGEMENT PLAN

### The Major Components of an Instructional Engagement Plan

As argued earlier, there are two major components involved in college instruction at its highest level: the seminar and topic survey (or more briefly, the seminar), and the instructor-student dialogue and course project (or more briefly, the dialogue). Before describing their use in detail, the following paragraphs will provide some notes on the nature of the seminar and dialogue of college instruction.

### The Seminar

The seminar consists of a series of class discussions based on study assignments. Typically, for each class session involving the seminar, while all students will be responsible for the study assignments, one student will take responsibility for reporting to the class his or her interpretation and assessment of the material and for leading the class in a discussion of the material assigned.

### The Dialogue

The dialogue, accompanied by a course project, involves a collaborative effort between instructor and student in an exploration of some aspect of the topic at hand. It provides the learner with an opportunity to collaborate with the instructor in an effort leading to the generation of original information in the field under study, and provides him or her with an opportunity to experience first hand the way in which workers in the field think about central aspects of the topic covered in the course.

The dialogue has a collaborative element in the sense that the student and instructor work together to carry out the study at hand, each participant contributing something from his or her own perspective to the effort. It also has a constructivist element in the sense that the participants generate the desired knowledge, skill or disposition through their interpretation of information generated through a process of inquiry. In addition, the dialogue has a meta-cognitive element in that the participants continually monitor and evaluate the way in which their thinking about the subject evolves throughout the inquiry process. Finally, the dialogue possesses a structure in the sense that it uses a framework for efficiently covering key elements of the process of inquiry.

For regular courses, the information generated through the process of inquiry of the dialogue and course project can be new to the student, although others may already possess the information. For courses involving the Bachelor's and Master's thesis or the doctoral dissertation, the information generated must be new to the field, although the degree of sophistication in the information-generating procedure and significance of the information generated is considerably higher for the Master's thesis than it is for the Bachelor's thesis – and considerably higher for the doctoral dissertation than it is for the Master's thesis. In any case, the value of the dialogue and course project for the student is that it affords him or her an opportunity to interact with his or her instructor in the process of inquiry, and in this way, to benefit from the collaborative and constructivist nature of the exercise.

The major difference between the seminar and dialogue has to do with their comparative scope and detail of coverage. The scope of the seminar and topic survey is relatively broad and its detail of coverage relatively limited, since its purpose is to provide the student with an overview of influential works in the field as well as with information in the field considered topical. For any given course, there will typically be at least as many seminar modules as course units or subtopics—and of necessity, due to time constraints, each module will be limited in the level of detail it can address. On the other hand, the scope of the dialogue and course project is relatively limited and its detail of coverage relatively broad, since the dialogue's purpose is to enable the learner to examine in depth some circumscribed aspect of the subject at hand. Through his or her participation in the dialogue and his or her conduct of the course project, the student addresses a subject limited in scope—the restriction enabling him or her to examine in detail the area he or she has chosen for investigation.

At times, some form of psychomotor skill (for example, playing a musical instrument, operating some sort of machinery or equipment) or cognitive process (for example, using an algorithm to solve a math problem) can best be addressed through the type of prescriptive instruction involved in deliberate practice (i.e., the instructor's demonstration of the target behavior, the student's enactment of the behavior, the instructor's feedback for fine-tuning of the student's skill).[1] By itself, this instructional mode, referred to in earlier parts of this text and described in detail in the companion book *The Psychology of Teaching and Learning* (Martinez-Pons, 2001), differs from the seminar and dialogue in its

---

[1] This form of instruction is also applicable when great disparities among students in a class emerge on pre-test performance and the instructor desires to raise all members of the class to a common level of preparedness before embarking on the activities of the seminar and dialogue.

relative lack of the discovery and collaborative activities that form intrinsic parts of the other two approaches. At any rate, at the highest levels of college teaching, the goal of instruction is to help the student to acquire affective, cognitive, or psychomotor processes that he or she can apply in critical areas of his or her life as an adult—and it is through the collaborative, constructivist activities involved in the seminar and dialogue that the instructor can best provide the student with the opportunity to achieve these ends. It is the seminar and dialogue whose use in college instruction will be described in the remainder of this chapter.

## Planning the Instructional Effort

The instructor can begin the development of the engagement plan by asking himself or herself the following questions:

1.  What do I want the students to do following instruction? (The instructional objectives should provide the answer to this question.)
2.  Do I need to use prescriptive instructional methodology to help the students to reach the instructional objectives? (The answer to this question will probably be in the affirmative if some sort of remedial work will be required for any of the students in the course, or if some sort of psychomotor or cognitive algorithmic process is involved in the objective of instruction.)
3.  How can I use the seminar and topic survey to help the students to reach the instructional objectives?
4.  How can I use the dialogue and course project to help the students to reach the instructional objectives?

Addressing these questions can enable the instructor to focus on the specific tasks that he or she will undertake to plan the instructional effort.

The tasks the college instructor undertakes in the planning of the instructional effort can be divided into two types: tasks involving the planning of activities preliminary to the seminar and dialogue, and tasks involving planning of the activities of the seminar and dialogue proper.

## Planning of Activities Preliminary to the Seminar and Dialogue

There are a number of activities the instructor must complete before undertaking those of the seminar or dialogue proper, and for which it is useful for him or her to plan in advance. These chores consist of the identification of core study materials and the preparation of study assignments.

### Identification of Core Study Materials

Core study materials involve basic information around which the course will revolve. Although at some point during a course students will need to locate on their own study material unique to their particular course interests, the instructor must in advance identify works around which main aspects of the course will orbit, and which all the students in the class will address. Such material typically involves readings, use of audiovisual media, and observation of processes related to the topic at hand.

*Readings*. As noted in Chapter 3, one of the major tasks college students undertake as they participate in the teaching-learning effort involves readings. Typically, reading material involves at least one textbook; and at times, any number of journal or newspaper articles, papers presented at professional conferences, and archival records.

Now no single literature type exists addressing any given topic of instruction; in fact, there are at least four major types of literature of interest to the college instructor as he or she plans the teaching-learning effort: the issue-oriented literature, the theory-oriented literature, the research-oriented literature, and the methodology-oriented literature.

*The Issue-Oriented Literature*. In the issue-oriented literature, authors discuss topics that the reader can interpret as meriting exploration. Newspaper articles and editorials, journal articles, and conference papers describing social issues are literature sources of possible areas for inquiry. In familiarizing students with the issue-oriented literature review, it is useful for the instructor to provide them with examples of works in this genre. For instance, he or she can provide students with a reading list of works proposing areas of study surrounding the subject of the course at hand, for example, school violence.

*The Theory-Oriented Literature*. In the theory-oriented literature, authors propose conceptual frameworks that can serve as guides in the exploration of the topic at hand. This literature offers theoretical models that the student can use in the formation of his or her conceptual framework for thinking about the topic at hand; it also offers variables or constructs that the student can use to expand his or her own conceptual framework. The conceptual framework the student develops on the basis of the theory-oriented literature can serve as the basis of research questions he or she will use to guide his or her study. In orienting students regarding this type of literature, it is useful to provide them with examples of works in this genre. For instance, assuming a course topic addressing school violence, the instructor can assign readings of several articles describing the authors' ideas regarding possible factors underlying school violence.

*The Research-Oriented Literature.* In the research-oriented literature, authors report the findings of investigations regarding some topic. The student can use these research findings as the bases for hypotheses as tentative answers to his or her research questions. In orienting students regarding the research-oriented literature, it is useful to provide them with examples of works in this genre. For instance, assuming a course topic addressing school violence, the instructor can assign an article reporting finding a relation of violent student behavior with such factors as home environmental violence and television violence.

*The Methodology-Oriented Literature.* In the methodology-oriented literature, workers describe modern research procedures that can be used for addressing the research questions and hypotheses at hand. This methodology can include descriptions of sampling techniques, research design, data-generation methods, and methods of data analysis relevant to the issue. In orienting students regarding this literature type, it is useful to provide them with examples of works in this genre. For instance, assuming a course topic involving school violence, the instructor can assign readings of chapters in a book on social research addressing methods of inquiry applicable to the topic.

The instructor must ensure that his or her students are familiar with these literature types and their function in the learning process; if they are, then he or she needs only remind his or her students of their use—otherwise, it may be necessary for him or her to devote some effort to familiarize his or her students with the different literature forms.

***Audiovisual Media.*** In addition to reading material, audiovisual media such as films, videotapes, audiotapes, and DVDs may contain information relevant to the objectives of the course, and the instructor may want to assign them as required study.

Whether the material the instructor chooses for assignment is found in the literature or in audiovisual media, there are three attributes he or she must consider in making his or her selection: the work's relevance to the instructional objectives at hand, the clarity of the work's exposition, and the work's adequacy for the readiness level of the students.

***Observations.*** In addition to reading and audiovisual material, the instructor can use observations, including ones with students as participants in the events of interest, as parts of the study assignments. An observation can take the form of a field assignment (for example, a student in, say, a sociology course visiting a prison and observing the social dynamics of some segment of the prison population, or a student in a physics class performing a laboratory experiment); or instructions to recall and describe some personal event (for example, a student recounting his or her first public speaking experience). The importance of a student's observations cannot be overemphasized, since they can often be more telling than other sources of information in providing the learner with insights into the dynamics of the issue at hand. The task assumes particular importance when the topic in question involves contextual elements that can be addressed only through attention to some process occurring at a time and place accessible only to the student.

A particularly comprehensive approach to observation assignments was described by Griffin (2002). In this approach, after identifying a critical incident he or she considers relevant to the topic at hand, the student analyzes it for content and for its implications for decision-making relative to the topic for discussion. The following is a generalized account of the steps in Griffin's (2002) approach to observation assignments:

1.  Describe the incident in terms of what happened, when it happened, where it happened, and who was involved. *In an example given by Griffin (2002), for an observation assignment related to the improvement of teaching practices in a teacher-education course, one student teacher reported a critical incident in which one of her pupils complained that she had been speaking too much in class and had not been allowing her pupils enough of an opportunity to actively participate in classroom activities.*

2.  Identify the feelings that were elicited by the incident and that give the event personal meaning for the student. *In the above example, the student teacher reported feeling surprised because she and another person with whom she had been team teaching had tried hard to make the material interesting to her pupils; she also reported feeling disappointed with herself*

*because she felt she should have known better than to devote so much time to lecturing, guilty when she realized that her classroom manner had been interfering with her students' learning, and grateful to her pupil for bringing the point home. These feelings propelled the teacher to reconsider her classroom behavior.*

3. Describe possible reasons for the incident, attempting to use the perspectives of participants in the event. *In the above example, the student teacher reported that she surmised that the complaint emanated from her pupil's desire to master the material, her pupil's conviction that she could master it only if she was involved in the teaching-learning process, and her pupil's frustration at being prevented from participating by the teacher's excessive involvement.*

4. Identify ways in which the incident fits into the topic for discussion. *In the above example, the student teacher argued that the incident fitted into the topic for discussion in that it highlighted the need for teachers to continually assess their teaching behavior to insure that it truly helps his or her students to benefit from the learning experience.*

5. Describe in detail the aspects of the subject at hand illustrated by the incident—not aspects of the incident itself but aspects of the subject at hand. *In the above example, one aspect of the topic at hand illustrated by the critical incident was the importance of going beyond instructional theory in one's teaching. Simply knowing something about theories of instruction is not enough to be successful as a teacher—it is also necessary to creatively translate theoretical concepts into real-life activities and to be able to gauge the activities' effectiveness—with feedback from students to identify areas for improvement.*

6. Describe implications of principles illustrated by the incident for decision-making, for action, for further study, etc. relative to the topic. *In the above example, the student teacher reported changing the way she plans and conducts her class activities. She now insures that she uses other teaching methods in addition to lecturing, structures, ways in which students can become actively involved in the teaching learning-process, and extensively uses on-going student feedback regarding the success of her teaching efforts.*

A special form of observation assignment involves laboratory work, alluded to earlier, in which the student carries out by himself or herself some scientific or technological procedure in order to experience first-hand, under highly controlled conditions, how the procedure works. According to Ehrlich (1963), laboratory work helps the student to master the principles and facts found in readings and lectures by presenting him or her with an opportunity to verify what he or she finds in textbooks and lectures, while ". . . sharpening your ability to observe and establish truths." (p. 168)

The major criteria for the use of any observation assignment are the specificity of the observation instructions (the purpose of the observation and the way the student will know whether the purpose has been met), and the relevance of the assignment to the instructional objectives at hand.

### Preparation of Study Assignments

Once the instructor has identified the materials that will serve as the study core for his or her course, he or she can decide which parts (book chapters, episodes of a television lecture series, the timing of field visits or laboratory assignments, recounting of personal experiences) he or she will assign for study, and the sequence in which the students will approach the various aspects of the material. This sequence will become part of the course syllabus, described at the end of this chapter.

### Planning the Activities of the Seminar and Dialogue

### Planning the Conduct of the Seminar

In planning for the conduct of the seminar, the instructor schedules the student presentations and discussions and prepares the seminar's activities.

**Scheduling of Class Presentations and Discussions**. The seminar involving a presentation and discussion by each individual student works best when class size does not exceed 15 members. The reason for this restriction has to do with time limitations, since each student presentation requires a certain amount of time (somewhere around 20 minutes) to serve its purpose, and the number of presentations that can be accommodated per session is limited by a number of factors, described below. This consideration becomes particularly important when the instructor intends to conduct class activities in addition to the seminar.

The number of discussions the instructor holds per class session will be a function of the number of students in the class, the number of sessions constituting the course and the time alloted per session. For a course spanning 14 sessions and involving, say, 10 students, the instructor can schedule one discussion per session with time left over for the covering of other course material. On the other hand, for a course spanning 14 sessions and involving, say, 28 students, the instructor will have to schedule an average of around 2 presentations per session—leaving less time for the covering of other course material. When class size makes individual presentations unfeasible, the instructor may be able to reach a compromise by dividing the class into small groups—and by then assigning a presentation to each group, each group member in turn taking responsibility for the presentation and discussion.

The instructor can take the following steps to schedule the seminar presentations:

1.  Determine the number of students in the class.
2.  Ascertain the number of class sessions to be held and the time per session.
3.  Schedule the presentation for each student or small group.

If there are more students or small groups presenting than there are class sessions, it will be necessary to assign two or more presentations for a certain number of sessions. The instructor can determine the number of presentations to schedule per session by dividing the number of sessions by the number of presenters.

**Planning the Seminar Activities by Reference to the Seminar's Structure**. The structure of the seminar and topic survey consists of four sequentially occurring sets of activities: student completion of study assignments, student-led class discussion, instructor recapitulation of salient discussion points, and student conceptual integration of learned material. To insure the success of the seminar, the instructor must be prepared to facilitate the students' efforts as they participate in this part of the instructional effort.

*Study Assignments*. In order to adequately participate in the activities of the seminar, students must complete study assignments (readings, observations) pertinent to the task. To facilitate learners' completion of study assignments, this author has found it useful to provide objectives for each task, and to provide guiding questions to help students to focus their attention on key points involved in the assignment—while linking the assignment objectives and guiding questions directly to the principal instructional objectives of the course. This author has also found it useful to require short written answers to the guiding questions to serve as the basis for each student's contribution to the class discussion. For example, for a session on the theorist B. F. Skinner in a graduate course on human motivation, this author assigned the guiding and discussion questions appearing in Figure 4.8 and he used student answers to these questions as the material for the class discussion for the corresponding course unit. (The author has found it expedient to use any number of the guiding questions as part of the final course examination, while alerting students to the fact that some of the questions will be included in the final exam. In the above example, this author selected Question 2 in Figure 4.8 as part of the final course examination.)

Often, particularly in seminars at the Master's and doctoral levels, the instructor will want his or her students to take a critical approach to assigned readings. For such cases, Figure 4.9 displays a format the instructor can provide his or her students for use as the basis

---

**CLASS DISCUSSION QUESTIONS FOR READING ASSIGNMENT\***
**REGARDING SKINNER'S POSITION ON THE STUDY OF**
**HUMAN BEHAVIOR**

1. What are four major tenets of Skinner's approach to the study of human behavior? Consider the following dichotomies in your answer: objectivity vs. introspection; the role of stimuli vs. consequents; individual vs. group analysis; intra-species vs. cross-species reinforcement laws.
2. What are some major criticisms of Skinner's position on theorization about human behavior? Consider the following issues in your response: The number of variables Skinner examines at one time; the use of inference in theory building; and the idea of cognitive processes to explain human behavior.
3. What would you say is the major difference between Bandura's and Skinner's approaches to the study of human motivation?
4. What advantages or disadvantages, if any, can you point to regarding Skinner's position on the study of human motivation?
5. How do you rate the structural integrity (differentiation, cohesiveness, comprehensiveness) of Skinner's work relative to human motivation?

\* Hall, C., Lindzey, G., & Campbell, J. B. (1988). Skinner's behaviorist position. *Theories of personality* (pp. 492–534). New York: John Wiley.

**Figure 4.8.   Class Discussion Questions for a Reading Assignment**

**Description of the Work at Hand**

I.      The work's title and the author's name
II.     The source (e.g., a journal article or newspaper article, a book, a conference presentation paper)
III.    The stated or implied purpose of the work, or the matter the author indicates he or she is addressing
IV.     The type of work the author presents (e.g., discussion of some issue, a theory, a research study, a work of fiction)
V.      Method of inquiry (essay, research, dialogue, etc.)
VI.     The information the author presents
VII.    Conclusions drawn by the author
VIII.   Relevance of the work to the instructional objectives

**Student's Assessment of the Work**

I.      Quality of the work
        A. Clarity of exposition of the work's various components
        B. Consistency among the work's various parts:

| | Purpose | Approach | Information | Conclusion |
|---|---|---|---|---|
| **Purpose** | Clarity of statement | Consistency | Consistency | Consistency |
| **Method of Inquiry** | | Clarity of description | Consistency | Consistency |
| **Information** | | | Clarity of description | Consistency |
| **Conclusion** | | | | Clarity of description |

        C. Comprehensiveness, or the degree to which the work accomplishes its stated or implied purpose

II.     Regardless of the student's overall evaluation, valuable idea or information he or she has derived from the work for thinking about the topic at hand

**Student's Recommendation for Future Activity in this Area**

**Student-Led Class Discussion**

**Figure 4.9.   Format for a Class Presentation of Review of Study Material**

of their reviews and class presentations. A key part of the format appearing in Figure 4.9 is the student's assessment of the consistency among the different parts of the work under discussion. This matter, addressed by the intersections of the matrix appearing in the figure, relates to the following questions:

1.  Does the approach taken by the author relate to the stated purpose of the study?
2.  Can the information presented by the author be said to be logically derived from the approach taken?
3.  Are the conclusions drawn by the author justified on the basis of the information presented?

A second key feature of the format appearing in Figure 4.9 involves the student's taking note of any valuable idea he or she can derive from the reading, *regardless of his or her overall evaluation of the work*.

***Class Discussion.*** While overseen by the instructor, the class discussion is led by a student who first reports to the class his or her review of the assigned material and then leads the class in a conversation revolving around the session's guiding questions.

During the discussion, the instructor allows as much freedom in the exchange as possible, intervening only to insure that the conversation serves the purpose of helping the students in their pursuit of the instructional objectives. Some latitude is permissible that may enable the discussion to range beyond what is relevant to the objectives but, in planning how much latitude to allow, the instructor must keep time limitations in mind.

***Instructor's Recapitulation.*** At the end of the discussion, the instructor shares with the class his or her interpretation of what has been said as well as his or her own ideas concerning the subject. He or she also points out the relevance of the discussion's outcomes to the instructional objectives of the course. In preparation for this part of the seminar, it is important for the instructor to insure his or her own familiarity with the material at hand as well as with issues or controversies that may attend the topic. In addition, it is useful for the instructor to be familiar with material not covered in the assignments that may nevertheless shed new insights into the topic. Finally, in preparation for the class discussion, it is also important for the instructor to collect and clarify his or her own thoughts about the subject—and to allow the possibility that changes will occur in his or her thinking in the course of the discussion.

***Integration by Each Student Into His or Her Conceptual Framework Relative to the Subject.*** As noted earlier, each student must be able to integrate whatever he or she gains from the seminar experience into his or her personal mental frameworks for thinking about the topic at hand. This integration can take the form of an expansion of the framework; elimination or modification of aspects of the framework; or reorganization of the framework's structure, in the form of the relations the student perceives to exist among its components. In preparing for this part of the seminar, the instructor can develop a description for the students of the way in which they can address these aspects of conceptual integration.

In focusing students' attention on the manner in which their thinking evolves during instruction, this author has found it useful to have them write what they think about the topic (ideas about basic principles, topical information, issues related to the topic) before engagement and following engagement—and to compare the two accounts. Invariably, students are impressed with the difference between their thinking about the subject before and following the seminar's activities.

In summary, the seminar and topic survey of the college teaching-learning effort consists of the following activities designed to help students to reach the instructional objectives at hand:

1. Student completion of study assignments
2. Student presentation of a review of assigned material, and conduct of a class discussion regarding the material
3. Recapitulation by the instructor of salient discussion points
4. Integration by each student of mastered material into his or her conceptual framework for thinking about the subject.

Careful planning by the instructor is important to insure that these activities lead to the reaching by the students of the instructional objectives for the course at hand.

## Planning the Conduct of the Dialogue and Course Project

Three parties play roles in the dialogue of college instruction: the educator, who, in Knowles' andragogical scheme (see Chapter 2 for a discussion of Knowles' work on andragogy), serves as guide in the process; a student who serves as the principal direct beneficiary of the exercise, and who is expected to pursue the objectives of instruction partly through his or her participation in the dialogue; and a study or support group whose function is to provide the student with the means for clarifying his or her thinking about the topic at hand in preparation for the instructor-student exchange. If the class is small (four to six students), then the entire class can serve as the support group for each of its members.

As with the seminar, the dialogue involving the instructor with each individual student works best when class size does not exceed 15 members. The reason for this limitation is that, to be effective, the instructor must devote a substantial amount of time to working with each individual student, and the time that he or she can devote to each participant is necessarily limited by class size. When class size renders the conduct of the dialogue on an individual basis unfeasible, the instructor may be able to reach a compromise by dividing the class into four- to six-member groups, and by then treating each small group as his or her interlocutor in the dialogue. In this case, the course project is undertaken as a small-group collaborative effort, and the rest of the class or segments of the rest of the class can serve as support for each small group.

Two sets of sessions are involved in the dialogue and course project: sessions involving each student's discussion with his or her support group, and sessions involving the student's dialogue with the instructor. Each instructor-student meeting, held out of class, is preceded by a meeting by the student with his or her support group.

**Scheduling of Dialogue Sessions**. In scheduling the dialogue sessions, it will be useful for the instructor to compare how much time he or she would like to devote to the dialogues with the actual amount of time he or she has available for the purpose. He or she can do so by first determining the total time for dialogue activities he or she will need given the number of students in the class, the time he or she would like to devote per dialogue session, and the number of sessions he or she would like to devote per student. The following formula is useful in calculating the total time necessary for the dialogues:

$$T = N\, L\, S,$$

where

$T$ = the total time to be devoted to the dialogue sessions
$N$ = number of students in the class
$L$ = length of time for each dialogue session
$S$ = number of dialogue sessions per student

Once he or she has determined $T$, the instructor can compare the amount of time he or she would like to devote to each session with the actual time he or she has available for the purpose. For example, assume that 15 students are enrolled in the course at hand, that the instructor plans to devote one hour to each dialogue session, and that he or she plans to hold 3 dialogue sessions with each student. For this course,

$$T = 15 \times 1 \times 3$$
$$= 45.$$

In this case, the total amount of time the instructor will need to devote to the dialogue portion of the course will be 45 hours. Assuming that, upon reflection, he or she decides that he or she does not have 45 hours available to devote for the purpose, the instructor can reconsider the length of time he or she will devote to each session or the number of sessions he or she will devote to each student. For example, with the instructor deciding to reduce the session length from 1 hour to 30 minutes and the number of sessions per student from 3 to 2, the total amount of time becomes

$$T = 15 \times .5 \times 2$$
$$= 15.$$

The instructor can manipulate the above equation to ascertain the length of time available per session given information at hand regarding the other terms in the equation:

$$L = T / (S\ N)$$

The instructor can also manipulate the above equation to ascertain the number of dialogue sessions available given information at hand regarding the other terms in the equation:

$$S = T / (L\ N)$$

Finally, the instructor can manipulate the original equation to determine the number of students he or she can accommodate given information about the other terms, as follows:

$$N = T / (L\ S)$$

It is important to note that these values are best seen as averages, since the amount of time the instructor devotes to each student will likely vary according to the nature of the student's project and learning needs.

Once he or she has reconciled the number of dialogue sessions with the other terms in the above equation, the instructor can schedule the times he or she will meet with each student (which students he or she will meet during each session can best be decided during the beginning of the course, after the instructor has ascertained the students' own schedules).

**Planning the Dialogue by Reference to the Dialogue's Structure.** The structure of the dialogue and course project consists of a number of sequentially occurring activities—and a process through which each of the activities is conducted. Figure 4.10 depicts this structure.

| Activity | Process | | | | |
|---|---|---|---|---|---|
| | | Student Preparation | | | |
| | Orientation by the Instructor | Individual Work: Readings, Observations, Interviews, Interpretation of Personal Experiences | Discussion with Support or Study Group | Instructor-Student Dialogue | Student's conceptual integration of the material and preparation of the Project Report* |
| Topic Selection | | | | | |
| Topic Focus | | | | | |
| Model Development | | | | | |
| Structural Integrity Test of the Model | | | | | |
| Instrumental Strength Test of the Model | | | | | |
| Research Questions | | | | | |
| Hypotheses | | | | | |
| Empirical Test of the Model | | | | | |
| Decision | | | | | |
| Identification of Implications for Further Study | | | | | |

*In the form of an oral presentation, a term paper, a thesis or a dissertation.

**Figure 4.10.    The Structure of the Instructor-Student Dialogue and Course Project**

*The Activities of the Dialogue and Course Project.* As shown in Figure 4.10, there are ten major activities involved in the dialogue and course project—beginning with the identification of an area of interest for inquiry, and ending with the identification of implications of findings for further study. To adequately plan each activity, the instructor must be familiar with its makeup and function. Appendix C discusses in detail the ten activities of the dialogue and course project.

*The Dialogue Process.* For each dialogue activity, a process exists that begins with an orientation of the students by the instructor regarding the nature of the work ahead and ends with the student's preparation of a report describing the course project that he or she completes as part of the dialogue process.

*1. Orientation by the Instructor.* It is important for the instructor to prepare a project orientation for the class, including an explanation of key criteria for selecting a topic for investigation; a description of the manner in which each student can prepare, through readings, observations, etc., to discuss the issue at hand; and a reiteration of how the student can integrate the dialogue experience into his or her conceptual framework for thinking about the topic.

2. *Student Preparation.* Because the success of the dialogue depends on the contributions the student makes to the process, preparation on his or her part is required that will enable him or her to contribute to the dialogue's success. First, the student prepares for the dialogue with information he or she gathers through such avenues as readings and observations. As he or she conducts these activities, the student identifies issues pertaining to the topic at hand, and he or she thinks of ways in which these issues can be addressed.

In preparation for the dialogue, the student also meets with his or her support group to discuss his or her thinking to date about the subject at hand. He or she presents his or her position to the group, and members of the group respond by posing questions for clarification, by raising issues regarding the validity of the student's thinking, and by offering suggestions for improvement. The student defends his or her position as he or she deems appropriate, and then uses the discussion experience to update his or her thinking about the matter. The instructor must be prepared to offer individual assistance as necessary as each student attempts to complete these activities.

3. *Instructor-Student Dialogue.* The student's dialogue with the instructor follows the same format as that of his or her discussion with his or her support group. He or she shares with the instructor the state of his or her thinking about the topic at hand, and the instructor responds by posing questions for clarification, by raising issues regarding the validity of the student's thinking, and by offering suggestions for improvement. The student defends his or her position as he or she deems appropriate, and then uses what he or she has gained from the interchange to update his or her thinking about the subject at hand.

As part of his or her role in the dialogue, in addition to responding to the student's position, the instructor endeavors to enable him or her to transfer dispositions, knowledge or skills gained through the dialogue and course project to situations different from that in which the effort takes place. Particularly in the case of application of learned material to novel tasks, because of obstacles to transfer often presented by contextual factors, successful application of learned material requires a certain form of self-regulatory behavior on the learner's part that will enable him or her to adjust to novel situations—partly by using already mastered material and partly by learning new material. Hence, in his or her planning of ways to promote transfer, it is important for the instructor to make provisions for the student's deliberate practice of self-regulatory transfer strategies.

    *4. Conceptual Integration of Material and Preparation of Project Report.* Finally, as the last step in the dialogue process, the student prepares a report of the investigation. This account can take such forms as an oral presentation, a term paper, a Master's thesis, or a doctoral dissertation and dissertation defence. In preparation to guide the student through this part of the course project, the instructor can develop written material describing the format of the report. Figure C3 shows one format the instructor can have at his or her disposal to guide the student in the writing of the report.

    An important point to be made concerning the seminar and dialogue of college instruction is that variations in their use departing from the instructional approach described above are possible. For one thing, it is possible to conduct the seminar leaving out some of the elements described in the preceding paragraphs. Figure 4.11 shows some

| Seminar Element | Scenario | | | |
| --- | --- | --- | --- | --- |
| | **A** | **B** | **C** | **D** |
| Completion of study assignment | x | x | x | x |
| Student's class report | x | x | | |
| Student-led class discussion | x | | x | |
| Instructor-led class discussion | | x | | x |
| Instructor's recapitulation of discussion points | x | x | x | x |
| Student's conceptual integration of covered material | x | x | x | x |

**Figure 4.11. Seminar Variations**

possible variations of the seminar component of college instruction. While different circumstances may of necessity call into play different variations appearing in Figure 4.11, Scenario A, that described above, is, in the judgment of this writer, the most powerful in enabling students to gain from the learning experience. Scenario D, lacking the element of a student report of assigned material and lacking the element of a student-led class discussion, would appear to be the least powerful.

What all seminar scenarios in Figure 4.11 share in common is that in each case students complete a study assignment, a class discussion of the assigned material takes place, the instructor recapitulates key discussion points, and each student integrates material covered into his or her conceptual framework for thinking about the topic at hand.

Regarding the dialogue and course project, it is possible to conduct these activities leaving out the use of a support group—although there can be little doubt that the use of a support group can greatly enhance the benefit the student derives from the activity.

Finally, it is possible to conduct the seminar and dialogue without the use of the course project, as happens in the case of the *practicum*, in which students practice in a real-life setting such as a classroom or hospital the craft they learn through the teaching-learning effort, and meet in a seminar setting as well as individually with the instructor to discuss their progress; and it is possible to conduct the dialogue and course project unaccompanied by a seminar, as happens in the *independent study course* in which typically only one student is enrolled. Still, barring these special circumstances, the combination of seminar and topic survey on the one hand, and the dialogue and course project on the other, offers, in this writer's view, the most powerful method for enabling students to master the material typically addressed at the highest levels of college instruction.

Thus, the college teaching-learning effort at its highest level consists of a seminar and topic survey whose purpose is to provide the student with an overview of influential and topical works in the field at hand; and an instructor-student dialogue and course project whose purpose is to provide the student with in-depth acquaintance with some key aspect of the subject, as well as with the way in which workers in the field think about the topic. In order to effectively conduct these two components of the college teaching-learning effort, the instructor must prepare through careful planning of preliminary activities and the activities constituting the structures of the seminar and dialogue.

## ENGAGEMENT MODULE TESTING AND ADJUSTMENT

Once the instructor has worked out the engagement module he or she will use in the teaching-learning effort, he or she can examine it to ascertain areas in need of adjustment. There are at least three ways in which the instructor can test the plan he or she has developed for engagement: through review and feedback by other instructors, through comparison with a model plan, and through small-scale tryout.

## Peer Review

In order to obtain their opinion concerning the likelihood of success of the module and to get their suggestions for improvement of the plan as necessary, the instructor can consult with peers who have had experience in instruction of the subject matter at hand.

## Comparison with a Model Lesson Plan

A useful way of assessing the likely success of a lesson plan is to compare it to an existing plan found to have worked well in the past. This method is especially helpful for identifying elements of a good lesson plan that the instructor may have overlooked. In such cases, the instructor can use the information gained through comparison to round out the engagement plan at hand.

## Small-Scale Tryout

In the absence of peers who can provide feedback concerning the quality of the lesson plan or of a model with which the lesson plan can be compared, the instructor can try out the lesson with a few students to identify areas in need of improvement. For example, he or she can assess the degree to which instructions are understandable to the students and the degree to which the students are able to keep up with the pacing of the presentation.

Once the instructor has developed the engagement plan, he or she can compare the objectives, assessment plan and activities of the instructional effort with the diagnostic findings regarding mental acuity and self-regulatory behavior—and develop remediation procedures as necessary to minimize any gaps between the engagement plan and the readiness level of the students.

## DEVELOPMENT OF REMEDIATION PROCEDURES ON THE BASIS OF DIAGNOSTIC FINDINGS RELATIVE TO THE INSTRUCTIONAL OBJECTIVES

For college students, remediation on the basis of diagnostic findings comes into play when deficiencies considered serious enough to interfere with their reaching of the present instructional objectives emerge in any of the following areas: efficiency in mental information processing; and self-regulation in emotional functioning, in the management of multiple social roles, in study activities, and in the transfer of learned material.

In extreme cases involving remediation, trained specialists such as college counsellors and reading and speech therapists may have to play leading roles in the planning and execution of the remedial effort. Also, if in the judgment of those in the best position to decide, a student can be helped to overcome learning-readiness deficiencies concurrently with regular academic work, the remedial effort can proceed at the same time that the student is engaged in the teaching-learning process. Otherwise, it may be necessary to conduct and complete the remedial work before the student begins participating in the instructional effort at hand.

In general, the process of remediation of deficiencies in learning readiness is the same in key respects as that of the teaching-learning effort described throughout this text; it involves, as a minimum, the following activities:

1. Formulation of the objectives to be sought through the remedial effort
2. Allocation of time and resources for the remedial effort
3. Development of formative and summative evaluation criteria and of methodology for the assessment of the success of the remedial effort
4. Development of remedial interventions.
5. Execution and formative evaluation of the remedial interventions.
6. Summative evaluation of the remedial effort.

## PREPARATION OF THE COURSE SYLLABUS

As a minimum, the course syllabus should contain the following items of information:

1. Course title
2. Office hours, office room and telephone numbers
3. College catalogue description including prerequisites and co-requisites
4. Remediation procedures to be used, if any
5. Objectives of the course
6. Preparation to meet the objectives
7. Assessment methodology
8. Testing policy
9. Unit Schedule
10. Reading schedule
11. Bibliography

Appendix J displays an example of a syllabus for an introductory course in educational research at the Master's level.

## PREPARATION OF CLASS ORIENTATION

At the beginning of a course, it is important for the instructor to explain to his or her students the nature of the activities to follow, to describe the manner in which students can prepare to participate in these activities, and to describe the way in which each learner can integrate his or her learning experience into his or her conceptual framework for thinking about the subject at hand. To prepare to conduct these activities, the instructor can develop a presentation, accompanied by printed material, addressing the issues involved. As a minimum, the presentation should cover the following points:

1. Objectives of the course
2. Testing procedures and grading policy
3. The nature of whatever prescriptive instruction is to follow
4. The nature of the seminar and course survey
5. The nature of the dialogue and course project
6. The nature of the review of study material; and the nature of observation assignments, if any

This author has found it useful, at the beginning of a class orientation, to allow time for the students to examine the course syllabus, and to then complete the orientation after addressing student questions regarding the syllabus.

In summary, the pre-engagement phase of college instruction, discussed in Part 2 of this work, involves the collection of information regarding needs to be addressed through the instructional effort and the readiness of instructor and students to undertake the teaching-learning effort; the development of assessment methodology and research procedure to gauge the success of the instructional effort; and the development of engagement methodology to enable students to reach the objectives of instruction.

Part 3 of the present work addresses the engagement phase of college instruction.

# PART 3

# THE ENGAGEMENT PHASE OF
# COLLEGE INSTRUCTION

In the engagement phase of college instruction, the educator implements the instructional plan he or she developed in the pre-engagement phase of the teaching-learning effort. Chapter 5 describes the engagement phase of the college instructional enterprise.

# Chapter 5

## Engagement

### INTRODUCTION

Chapter 3 discussed the activities the instructor undertakes to prepare to engage the student in the teaching-learning effort. Chapter 5 discusses the actual engagement of the student in this undertaking; in doing so, it considers four aspects of the engagement phase of instruction: appraisal of the situation in which instruction is about to take place, engagement of the student in the learning process, formative evaluation of the engagement effort, and crisis intervention.

### SITUATIONAL APPRAISAL

Situational appraisal involves a last minute check to ensure that conditions in the learning setting are likely to promote the success of the teaching-learning effort about to take place. There are at least five aspects of the learning setting for which the instructor conducts last-minute appraisal activities: *administrative support; school staff support; the physical setting of the engagement effort; availability of instructional materials;* and *student and instructor readiness to embark on the teaching-learning effort.*

## Institutional Support

### Administrative Support

Administrative support involves help lent by school administrators to the instructor as he or she carries out the teaching-learning effort. Areas in which the instructor needs the support of school administrators are: guidance concerning performance expectations; backing in disciplinary cases; backing in dealings with parents, the community, and upper echelons in the school system; ensuring the availability of school supplies; and encouragement and recognition of good performance.

In addition, administrators can support the teaching-learning effort by insuring the quality of security and first aid services, and by insuring the existence of clear fire routes and fire evacuation plans. The degree to which administrators provide this form of support is the degree to which they can be said to contribute to the success of the teaching-learning effort (Smith, Neisworth & Greer, 1978).

### Staff Support

A security force, a student advisement center, and a first aid station are typically found on the typical college campus. It is important for the instructor to be familiar with the range of services offered and the persons performing these services in order to access them as the need arises—and to insure that he or she has established lines of communication with these individuals in case the need arises to appeal to them for aid.

## Physical Environment

The quality of the physical environment of the instructional setting can affect the success of the teaching-learning effort. In terms of environmental health hazards, cosmetic and aesthetic elements of the environment, comfortable seating, and adequate lighting, the instructor must take last-minute steps to insure that the state of the setting's physical plant is conducive to the success of the teaching-learning effort. In addition, a number of elements of the physical environment were cited by Smith, Neisworth and Greer (1978) as targets for situational assessment: designation of special places where students can go for isolation, quiet, self-reward, independent work, and private discipline; movable furniture for grouping purposes; and storage facilities for students to put away personal effects and study materials.

## Instructional Materials

The instructor must ensure that visual aids, textbooks, handouts, lesson plan, student writing materials, etc., are on hand before beginning the engagement effort. A checklist developed well in advance of engagement can be of great help in ensuring that the necessary materials are on hand before beginning the engagement process.

## Students

A last-minute check by the instructor is important to ensure that his or her students are present and prepared to participate in the engagement process. Three aspects of student preparation are especially relevant at this point: a reasonably clear idea on the student's part of that which he or she is to achieve through the learning experience, his or her motivation to undertake the learning task, and his or her psycho-physiological state at the time of engagement.

### Clear Understanding of the Learning Goals

There are two levels at which the student's awareness of that which he or she is to gain from the learning experience becomes relevant as engagement begins. First, more generally, it is important for the learner to understand the need on his or her part that the target of instruction is meant to address, since an idea of the connection between the two can provide him or her with a frame of reference for judging the relevance of the material he or she encounters during engagement. For example, instruction concerning the multiplication of fractions can become meaningful to the student if he or she has experienced a desire to develop this skill and also sees the relevance of the present assignment relative to this wish. More specifically, it is important for the student to be aware of those subskills he or she must master as he or she sets out to meet the instructional objectives at hand. For example, if he or she understands that mastery of multiplication of fractions presupposes mastery of subskills in fraction addition and common denominator calculations, the student will be in a favorable position to attend to instruction when it takes place addressing these two prerequisite skills.

## Motivation

Two aspects of motivation may be important to consider at this point. One involves the possibility of lowered motivation to *engage* in the learning task, and the other involves the possibility of heightened motivation to *avoid* the material to be covered.

**Lowered Motivation to Engage in the Learning Task**. An aspect of motivation that may be important to consider before engagement begins is the possibility that the student will lack the necessary incentive to undertake the task at hand simply because he or she lacks a sense of personal significance regarding the material. In such a case, it may be possible to point out the short- and long-term importance of the material for the student. For example, the instructor can note that mastering the present material will enable the student to master more complex material to follow and thus raise the likelihood of performing well in the course; or that mastering the present as well as subsequent material will enable the student to attain a high academic grade point average—or to eventually pursue the kind of work to which he or she aspires as an adult.

**Heightened Motivation to Avoid the Learning Task**. It is possible that, due to task-anxiety generated through past aversive experiences with the topic or because of a lack of confidence in his or her ability to master the present material, the student will experience a desire to avoid the learning task at hand. If such is the case, it may be necessary for the instructor to undertake last-minute anxiety-reduction activities before proceeding with the engagement effort—or to persuade the student that he or she is capable of mastering the task, if only he or she persists in using the right learning strategies for the purpose.

## Instructor

The instructor's mood, alertness, and enthusiasm for the topic at hand will significantly influence his or her performance in class. Tension-reducing deep-breathing and relaxation exercises can be useful at this point to prepare to enter into the teaching-learning effort fully engaged in the proceedings.

## PRE-TESTING

It is important for the instructor to conduct whatever pre-testing he or she will do on the first day of class, since a certain amount of time will be involved in the conduct of any necessary remedial intervention on the basis of pre-test findings. The purpose in pre-testing is to determine whether some sort of intervention is necessary to bring the class as a group to the entry level necessary for the present engagement effort to begin.

## INTERVENTION ON THE BASIS OF PRE-TEST FINDINGS

When great disparities emerge between students in pre-test performance, it may become necessary to exert some effort to minimize the differences. When this happens, the ideal approach is to develop individualized instruction to bring students at lower entry levels to the level of the higher-achieving students; when limitations in time or resources make complete individualization unfeasible, it may be possible to group students in terms of common pre-test patterns—and to then develop instruction to raise groups at lower entry levels to the levels of the higher-achieving groups. When timely, effective intervention is not possible to prepare a student for participation in the engagement effort at hand, the instructor may have no choice other than to recommend to the student that he or she drop the course and undertake it again later, after preparing for it through some form of remedial work.

Once the instructor has insured that the students in his or her class are at the entry level necessary for their participation in the teaching-learning effort, he or she can implement the engagement plan for the course.

## ENGAGEMENT-PLAN IMPLEMENTATION

The reader will recall that, in general terms, the engagement plan involves an orientation by the instructor concerning the activities to follow, a seminar and topic survey, and an instructor-student dialogue and course project. Figure 5.1 summarizes the activities involved in these components of engagement.

The details of each of these aspects of the plan constitute the activities of the engagement effort.

Four key elements of module-implementation are of interest at this point: implementation of the engagement plan, the instructor's conduct during engagement, formative evaluation of the engagement process, and crisis intervention.

---

**Orientation**

1. Objectives of the course
2. The nature of whatever prescriptive instruction is to follow
3. The nature of the seminar and course survey
4. The nature of the dialogue and course project
5. The nature of the review of study material

**Seminar and Topic Survey**

1. Student-led class discussion of assigned material
2. Recapitulation by the instructor of salient discussion points
3. Integration by each student of mastered material into his or her conceptual framework for thinking about the subject

**Dialogue and Course Project**

1. Orientation by the Instructor
2. Instructor-Student Dialogue
3. Project report

## Figure 5.1.  Summary of the Engagement Plan

---

### Instructor's Engagement Behavior

In over 15 years of observation and evaluation of instructor classroom performance at both the school and college levels, the more successful workers this writer has observed have followed what amounts to basic principles of social cognitive learning theory: modeling, encouragement, facilitation and rewarding. These behaviors were described in detail by Martinez-Pons (1999, 2002).

### Modeling

Modeling involves the instructor's enactment of the cognitive, affective or psychomotor process addressed in the instructional objectives and taught during the engagement effort.

### Encouragement

Whenever a student attempts to enact complex behavior for the first time, he or she is unlikely to do so with perfect accuracy—and he or she runs the risk of experiencing some discouragement in the face of early failure. For this reason, in the early phases of learning, students need encouragement to persist in their learning effort as they originally fail to meet performance criteria. At the very least, it is important for the instructor to refrain from doing or saying anything, and to prevent others, from doing or saying anything (showing impatience, taking the spotlight away from the student and enacting the behavior for him or her, making invidious comparisons with others more proficient at the task, ascribing the early failure to lack of ability rather than to lack of practice in using the right approach) that may contribute to the discouragement.

**Facilitation**

Sometimes, modeling and encouragement on the part of the instructor are not enough to enable a student to master new material. Often, it is necessary to take time to facilitate the student's learning effort by offering concentrated guidance through the forms of activities described by Collins et al. (1989) in their method of apprenticeship learning. In this approach, after modeling the behavior in detail and explaining its subtleties to the student, the instructor offers feedback and suggestions on the basis of the student's attempts to replicate the behavior; encourages the student to "talk his or her way through" the behavior to develop a better understanding of it; and encourages him or her to go beyond the behavior mastered and explore ways of applying it to other aspects of his or her academic work.

**Rewarding**

As is well-known, behavior that is rewarded is likely to recur and behavior that is punished or not rewarded is unlikely to recur. This rule applies to adult learners as well as to school-age students, and so, the college instructor must be prepared to reward his or her students when they attempt to enact the behavior at hand, when they persist in this attempt, and when they succeed in the attempt.

An important rule that applies during engagement is that, in order to try to capitalize on the thinking and effort that went into its development, the instructor must begin the teaching-learning endeavor with implementation of the plan he or she originally developed: if in the course of engagement the need arises to modify elements of the plan, it is important to know the exact part in need of modification; but if he or she does not at first adhere to the original plan, the instructor may find it difficult if not impossible to determine with confidence which part of the process is in need of modification—or how such modification may impact on other elements of the process.

This last issue leads to the next point concerning engagement: the implementation of an instructional module seldom proves to be straightforward. First, rather than delivering the information exactly as planned, the successful instructor continually adjusts the content, sequence, intensity, and pace of the engagement activities in response to changing conditions. Second, crises during engagement tend to arise to which the instructor must attend to ensure the likelihood of the success of the teaching-learning effort. In order to ascertain whether adjustments are necessary in the course of engagement, the instructor conducts an ongoing, formative evaluation of the effort progress.

## FORMATIVE EVALUATION

It is the purpose of formative evaluation to enable the instructor to ascertain whether what is taking place in the teaching-learning setting is likely to lead to the attainment by the students of the objectives of instruction.

### Targets of Formative Evaluation

Targets of formative evaluation include student performance, teacher performance, and the quality of support provided by school administrators and staff. In each case, the instructor continually monitors the performance of the different parties involved and, when detecting any problem, takes steps to address it.

### Formative Evaluation Methods

There are a number of ways in which the instructor can monitor the progress of the engagement effort. Some of the more widely used are *observations*, *tests and quizzes*, and *consultations*.

### Observations

Observations are notes the instructor makes concerning critical incidents that occur during the process of engagement.

### Quizzes

The instructor can use quizzes to ascertain whether students are mastering skills specified in the objectives of instruction. In cases in which mastery has not occurred, the instructor can ascertain the reason and take corrective action.

## Consultations

Consultations are conversations the instructor conducts with students and others to ascertain how they feel the engagement effort is progressing. The instructor can evaluate concerns raised by students and others during consultation using the issues-analysis framework depicted in Tables 5.1–3. He or she can then address those concerns he or she deems legitimate and relevant to the likelihood of the success of the engagement effort.

## CRISIS INTERVENTION

Often in the course of formative evaluation, the instructor will note conditions that threaten to impede learning and require some sort of action to ensure the success of the teaching-learning effort in progress. This type of activity is termed *crisis intervention*. The following pages discuss the topic in terms of the manner in which *crisis* is defined; the use of the scientific method in crisis intervention; and types of classroom crises the instructor is likely to encounter, along with applicable crisis intervention procedures.

### Definition of *Crisis*

A crisis is the occurrence of any event in the teaching-learning setting that threatens to interfere with students' reaching of the objectives of instruction.

### Types of Crisis

Two general types of crisis can occur in the teaching-learning setting: *crises originating with students* and *crises originating with the instructor.*

### Crises Originating with Students

There are at least six major forms of student-originated crisis the college instructor is likely to encounter in his or her classroom. These crises involve decrements in student functioning relative to the learning-readiness areas discussed in Chapter 3: *academic self-regulation, emotional functioning, mental efficiency*, and *multiple-social-role management*; and, in addition, *interaction with peers* and *health issues*. Although a student may have shown adequate functioning levels in each of these areas, sudden problems may arise during engagement due to changing conditions in the student's life. Table 5.1 displays a form the instructor can use to record student-originated crises. The instructor can use this form to keep a record of any specific problem encountered (under the column heading *Critical Incident(s)*), the level of seriousness of the problem (under the column heading *Seriousness*), and the degree to which the problem is resolved during engagement. If this level of interference is high enough, it may be necessary for the instructor to do something to address the problem; in cases in which the instructor cannot do so, he or she may have to refer to an outside source for help in addressing the issues.

Of special interest regarding the forms of student-originated crisis appearing in Table 5.1 is that of decrement in that aspect of self-regulatory behavior involving self-efficacy. This issue is important because, forming an integral part of motivation, self-efficacy often underlies a student's inability or unwillingness to overcome obstacles to his or her learning efforts. Because of its fundamental role in the occurrence of instructional crises, it will be considered in some detail.

**Decrement in Self-Efficacy (DSE).** Self-efficacy involves one's belief that one can successfully perform some task (Bandura, 1977b, 1986). According to Bandura, self-efficacy serves three important motivational functions in learning: first, it motivates the student to undertake courses of action he or she might not otherwise consider. Second, it motivates the student to persist at some task to the point of mastery. Third, it motivates the student to apply what he or she has learned to novel situations.

A number of factors influence the development of self-efficacy: one's prior successes or failures; the success or failure of others with whom one identifies; and of particular importance, attributions made by others regarding one's successes or failures (Bandura, 1986). Decrement in self-efficacy (DSE) involves the feeling that one is incapable of performing some task. A key element of DSE is the attribution of lowered efficacy to lack of ability rather than to the use of the wrong strategy or to lack of persistence in attempts to master some task.

Of particular interest regarding DSE is what often proves to be its social origin. As noted earlier, an effective instructor is one who models desired behavior for a student, encourages the student's continued attempts at enactment of the behavior, facilitates the student's attempts at mastery of the behavior, and rewards the student's attempts at mastery. A risk for the onset of DSE occurs in the early phases of learning: in general, it is unlikely that a person can completely succeed the first time he or she attempts to enact some complex behavior. An important source of DSE at this point can take the form of someone persuading the learner that the reason he or she has failed to accurately reproduce the behavior is lack of ability, rather than lack of proper strategy usage. (The opposite, encouragement, would involve persuading the person that "failure" is natural in the early phases of learning—that if he or she persists in attempts at "fine tuning" of his or her effort, he or she will succeed.)

Major differences exist between the DSE concept and the concept of learned helplessness (LH) propounded by Peterson et al. (1993): first, while the former takes the condition's possible social origin into account, the latter considers only the facts of non-contingency and the spontaneous attribution to lack of ability; second, while LH assumes that some form of aversive experience occurring randomly, independently of one's actions, generates the feeling of helplessness, DSE stipulates no aversive experience in the development of decrement in self-efficacy— positing that often, only a persuasive message by another person is necessary to induce one to attribute failure to lack of ability on one's part. The instructor can deal with DSE by first identifying and neutralizing its source; and second, enabling the student to begin making attributions for failure to personal effort or ineffective strategy usage rather than to lack of ability.

Thus, student-generated crises involve behavior threatening to interfere with the success of the teaching-learning effort. Six forms of student-generated crisis are *academic self-regulation, emotional functioning, mental efficiency*, and *multiple-social-role management*; and, in addition, *interaction with peers* and *health issues*. Each crisis form calls for its own unique form of intervention, and the college instructor skillful in addressing them will be in a favorable position to ensure the success of the teaching-learning effort even when such crises arise.

Table 5.1 displays an instrument the instructor can use for the formative evaluation of student behavior during the engagement phase of instruction. The instructor can use this record later, during the post-engagement phase of instruction, to decide on any remediation steps to be taken before initiating any subsequent engagement activity.

## Crises Originating with the Instructor

Often, the instructor himself or herself can be instrumental in the incidence of crises during the engagement phase of instruction. In general, the ways in which instructors can induce crises in the college classroom fall into two categories: crises involving student motivation, and crises involving student learning.

**Table 5.1. Student Observation Record**

| Area | Critical Incident(s) | Degree of interference with learning | | | | Degree of resolution of the problem | | |
|---|---|---|---|---|---|---|---|---|
| | | *Low 1* | *2* | *3* | *High 4* | *None 1* | *Part 2* | *Total 3* |
| Health issues | | | | | | | | |
| Academic self-regulation *motivation (self-efficacy, outcome expectations)* | | | | | | | | |
| *goal setting* | | | | | | | | |
| *strategy usage* | | | | | | | | |
| *self-monitoring* | | | | | | | | |
| Emotional Functioning | | | | | | | | |
| Mental acuity *acquisition* | | | | | | | | |
| *retention* | | | | | | | | |
| *utilization* | | | | | | | | |
| Interactions with peers | | | | | | | | |
| Multiple Social Roles | | | | | | | | |
| Other | | | | | | | | |

**Instructor-Induced Crises Involving Student Motivation.** There are at least eight ways in which instructors can decrease student motivation to participate in the teaching-learning effort:

1. Displaying a lack of enthusiasm for the topic at hand
2. Failing to keep appointments with students
3. Being late for class or failing to appear in class
4. Departing without good reason from specifications of the course syllabus
5. Displaying hostile behavior toward students
6. Failing to recognize student contributions to class activities
7. Pointing out weaknesses without offering guidance for improvement
8. Making invidious comparisons among students
9. Failing to maintain a professional classroom atmosphere
10. Attributing early failure to lack of ability or integrity rather than to improper strategy use

**Instructor-Induced Crises Involving Student Learning Processes.** Callahan et al. (1998) noted upward of 50 mistakes instructors can make that impede students' learning. Among them are *using sketchy lesson plans* that fail to attend to individual differences; *spending too much time (over 30 seconds) with one student or one group and neglecting the rest of the class; beginning a new activity before gaining students' attention; manifesting nervousness and anxiety*; and *ignoring student thinking processes and concentrating only on correct answers when reading student papers.*

Table 5.2 is an instrument the instructor can use for the formative evaluation of his or her own performance during the engagement phase of instruction, in order to keep a record of any specific problem encountered (under the column heading *Critical Incident(s)*), the seriousness of the problem (under the column heading *seriousness*), and the degree to which the problem is resolved during engagement. The instructor can use this record later, during the post-engagement phase of instruction, to decide on any remediation steps to be taken before initiating any subsequent engagement efforts.

A second set of what may be termed instructor-induced crises related to student learning involves the effectiveness of the methods and procedures the instructor uses in the pre-engagement and engagement phases of instruction. The instructor must ask whether the needs assessment, diagnostic procedures, instructional objectives, task analysis, assessment methodology, engagement plan and situational-appraisal methods designed for instruction are serving their purpose—and if not,

**Table 5.2. Instructor-System Observation Record**

| Area | Critical Incident(s) | Degree of interference with learning | | | | Degree of resolution of the problem | | |
|---|---|---|---|---|---|---|---|---|
| | | Low 1 | 2 | 3 | High 4 | None 1 | Part 2 | Total 3 |
| Instructor's efficacy *knowledge of subject taught* | | | | | | | | |
| *pedagogical skills* | | | | | | | | |
| Instructor's commitment to the teaching effort | | | | | | | | |
| Instructor's teaching mode *modeling* | | | | | | | | |
| *encouraging* | | | | | | | | |
| *facilitating* | | | | | | | | |
| *rewarding* | | | | | | | | |
| Administrataive support | | | | | | | | |
| Staff support | | | | | | | | |
| Other | | | | | | | | |

**Table 5.3 Procedural Observation Record**

| Area | Problem in design or execution | Degree of interference with learning | | | | Degree of resolution of the problem | | |
|---|---|---|---|---|---|---|---|---|
| | | *Low* *1* | *2* | *3* | *High* *4* | *None* *1* | *Part* *2* | *Total* *3* |
| Needs assessment | | | | | | | | |
| Diagnostic procedures | | | | | | | | |
| Instructional objectives | | | | | | | | |
| Task analysis | | | | | | | | |
| Assessment methodology | | | | | | | | |
| Engagement procedure | | | | | | | | |
| Situational appraisal | | | | | | | | |
| Other | | | | | | | | |

what the instructor can do to rectify the situation. Table 5.3 is an instrument the instructor can use to keep a record of problems encountered in these areas, their seriousness and the degree of success in attempts at their resolution.

## SUMMARY

In summary, in the engagement phase of instruction the educator makes a last-minute check of the conditions under which instruction is to take place, engages the student in the teaching-learning effort, conducts formative evaluation of the proceedings, and intervenes in cases in which crises arise that may threaten to interfere with the attainment of the objectives of instruction. In the next phase of the instructional process, the instructor assesses the success of the instructional activities and takes steps to resolve whatever issues emerge in the evaluation.

# PART 4

# THE POST-ENGAGEMENT PHASE OF COLLEGE INSTRUCTION

After completing the engagement phase of college teaching, the instructor determines the success of the endeavor and attends to whatever areas for improvement he or she identifies through the evaluation effort. The form of assessment that comes following engagement is termed *summative evaluation*; and the action the instructor takes to address areas for improvement is termed *post-engagement remediation*, or more simply, *remediation*. Chapter 6 describes the process of summative evaluation, and Chapter 7 discusses the process of remediation.

# Chapter 6

## Summative Evaluation

### INTRODUCTION

Chapter 6 describes the process of evaluation following the engagement phase of instruction. First, it examines the way in which summative evaluation is conceptualized; then, after looking at the targets and sources of summative evaluation, the chapter describes the methodology and process of the summative evaluation effort.

### THE NOTION OF SUMMATIVE EVALUATION

The term *summative evaluation* can be used in one of two ways. First, it can be used to refer to the appraisal of faculty performance in general, including teaching, record of publications, service to the institution, and service to the community (Cohen & McKeachie, 1980; Reig & Waggoner, 1995). In this sense of the term, summative evaluation is used administratively for the purpose of retention, pay raises, tenure, and promotion.

The second way in which the term "summative evaluation" can be used, and the way in which it is used here, is restricted to an appraisal of the success of a specific instructional effort. In this sense of the term, summative evaluation is used pedagogically for the purposes of student, instructor and institutional remediation following completion of the instructional effort.

For the purpose of summative evaluation, Figure 6.1 shows a hypothetical model addressing the relations that exist between college instruction and expected student outcomes. The model appearing in Figure 6.1 stipulates that institutional support is an important condition for effective instruction to take place; that effective instruction is an important condition for effective student learning behavior to occur; that this behavior is an important condition for the effective acquisition of instructional material; that effective acquisition is an important condition for effective retention of the material; that effective retention is important for the generation on the students' part of new cognitive, affective or psychomotor information or processes; and that generation of new information is an important condition for the application of learned material.

It is the purpose of summative evaluation to ascertain the degree to which students have attained the instructional objectives related to the student outcomes appearing in Figure 6.1, and the extent to which institutional support and the quality of instruction have contributed to these outcomes. Given high correlations among the linked factors, it may be assumed that low performance on any of the outcomes can be traced back to antecedent factors in the model. In this way, the model can serve as a diagnostic framework for identifying the causes of lowered course performance when it occurs.

Four aspects of summative evaluation will be addressed in the following pages: the targets of summative evaluation, sources of summative evaluation, evaluation methodology, and the assessment process for the various targets of summative evaluation.

## THE TARGETS OF SUMMATIVE EVALUATION

The primary target of summative evaluation involves the question of whether students have reached the instructional objectives at hand. When the answer to this question is in the negative, the reason for the failure becomes the focus of attention, and secondary targets of summative evaluation become the student's learning behavior, the quality of instruction, and the support the institution has lent to the instructional effort.

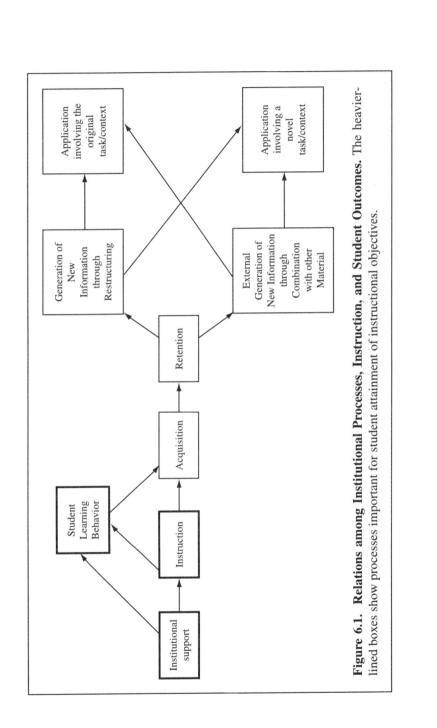

**Figure 6.1. Relations among Institutional Processes, Instruction, and Student Outcomes.** The heavier-lined boxes show processes important for student attainment of instructional objectives.

## SOURCES OF SUMMATIVE EVALUATION

Scholars have cited several sources of information in summative evaluation: the instructor himself or herself, other instructors, administrators, researchers, trained evaluators, independent observers, and students (Dwyer & Stufflebeam, 1996; Kaufman & Madden, 1980; Theall & Franklin, 1991). Although evaluation by administrators and students will be touched upon in the following pages, the major source of summative evaluation discussed will be the instructor; the usefulness of administrators and students as evaluation sources will be briefly considered first.

### The Administrator as Source of Summative Evaluation

According to Dwyer and Stufflebeam (1996), intuitive appeal has been the major criterion governing the acceptance or rejection of assessment methodology used by administrators. Little or no technical information exists regarding the validity or reliability of this methodology. What little research exists in support of the methodology, it exists mainly in the form of *meta-analytical* studies that aggregate the results of investigations differing fundamentally in conceptualization and research design. Moreover, the prescribed teaching method administrators typically use as basis for evaluation often penalizes the creative instructor who uses an innovative approach to meet situational demands. For these reasons, in the view of Dwyer and Stufflebeam (1996), the value of administrators as source of summative evaluation is limited.

### The Student as Source of Summative Evaluation

Concerning the suitability of students as source of summative evaluation, the literature during the past several decades has shown inconsistent findings. For example, while Aubrecht (1979) and Cashin (1991) reported literature reviews attesting to the validity, reliability and usability of student evaluation of faculty, Owen (1976), Morrow (1977), and Charles (1978) expressed concern with the objectivity, validity, reliability and utility of instruments used for student ratings of instructor performance. Morrow (1977) and d'Apollonia and Abrami (1997) cited research pointing to important limitations in the approach.

Ruskai (1996) alluded to college faculty opposition to student evaluation of teaching:

Many    experienced    faculty    question    the    reliability    of    student evaluations as a measure of teaching effectiveness and worry that they may have counter-productive effects, such as contributing to grade inflation, discouraging innovation, and deterring instructors from challenging students. (p. 308)

In this author's view, the inconsistent findings regarding student ratings of the quality of instruction may have more to do with the design of evaluative efforts than with any inherent property of student evaluation of instructor performance. The following are some factors that, in the views of this writer and others, may engender student differences in instructor ratings independently of instructional quality: student learning readiness, student objectivity, questionnaire specificity, and instrument types used. In what follows, each factor is accompanied by a way in which its confounding effect may be reduced.

## Student Learning Readiness

Student differences in learning readiness may influence their responses to evaluation questions and thus confound the findings. Consider for example the following question:

> *How would you rate the difficulty of the reading material regarding solution of quadratic equations used in this course?*
>
> *Too easy*          *Appropriate*          *Too difficult*
>    $-3$   $-2$   $-1$   $0$   $1$   $2$   $3$

While students with a high level of learning readiness may have found the material very easy, students with a low level of learning readiness may have found it very difficult. Averaging their ratings would produce a false indication that the students found the material's level of difficulty appropriate—diluting the rating's value in helping to determine the reading material's difficulty level. One way to control for this artifact is to take into account the learning readiness of the students before engagement, and to then separately examine and utilize the responses according to learning readiness groupings.

## Student Objectivity

Some students may lack objectivity in responding to a given query. For example, it is possible that a student who has received a low grade from the present instructor in a previous class may unfavorably rate the instructor's ability to communicate effectively, although by all accounts the instructor's ability in this respect may be high. The instructor can estimate the degree to which a halo effect is at play by correlating information regarding such conceptually mutually independent properties. After controlling for possible confounding effects, the instructor can consider a high correlation between such mutually independent elements indicative of a halo effect.

## Question Specificity

Lack of specificity in the questions posed for evaluation may negatively impact on the usefulness of responses. It is well known that when eliciting student self-ratings of academic efficacy, general statements such as "I can do well in college" are not as predictive of academic achievement as specific statements such as "I can earn an A in this chemistry course" (Bandura, 1998)—and the same may hold true for student ratings of instruction when queries are posed in general terms. One way to avert this condition is to pose queries that refer to specific features of the behavior enacted by the instructor or of the materials and procedures utilized in the engagement effort—and then to specifically inquire of the student how instrumental he or she believes the item was in helping him or her to master the material. Figure 6.2 shows a general framework for the development of student queries for the summative evaluation of instruction. In this table, the *Item* column contains major groups of

| | **Response Format** | | | | |
|---|---|---|---|---|---|
| **Item** | *Greatly interfered with my mastering of the material* <br> *1* | *Somewhat interfered with my mastering of the material* <br> *2* | *Had nothing to do with my mastering of the material* <br> *3* | *Somewhat facilitated my mastering of the material* <br> *4* | *Greatly facilitated my mastering of the material* <br> *5* |
| List of specific instructor behaviors | | | | | |
| List of specific procedural features | | | | | |
| List of specific materials used | | | | | |

**Figure 6.2. Framework for Development of Student Queries for Summative Evaluation of Instruction**

elements for evaluation, and the *Response Format* columns show a response format the student can use to gauge the degree to which each item in a questionnaire served to enable him or her to master the material covered during engagement.

## Types of Instruments Used

Bangura (1994) argued that the use of survey questionnaires limits the validity of student evaluation of instruction because such methodology is impersonal, lacks opportunities for probing, suppresses discourse as a rich source of information by presenting fixed-choice and yes-no questions, and disregards respondents' social and cultural backgrounds in their interpretation of the questions. As an alternative to questionnaires, the author suggested the use of *focus group interviews*, which enable the evaluator to explore in depth connections between student perceptions and performance.

## The Instructor as Source of Summative Evaluation

While it may be possible for the instructor to use information provided by administrators and students for the purpose of summative evaluation, ultimately it will be his or her own judgment, based on the information available, which will serve as the basis for his or her remediation effort in the post-engagement phase of instruction.

In this writer's view, aside from procedural issues and issues of validity and reliability of the assessment instruments used, the question concerning administrators', students', and instructors' suitability as sources of summative evaluation revolves around that aspect of the instructional enterprise that each is best suited to evaluate. While under special circumstances each source may be able to address every aspect of instruction, this level of comprehensiveness cannot be expected to obtain for all sources under normal circumstances. Figure 6.3 shows those targets of evaluation each source is best qualified to assess under normal conditions.

It is argued that how suitable someone can be as a source of evaluation is a function of his or her proximity of contact with the target of evaluation. As suggested in Figure 6.3, the administrator, being part and parcel of the college's supportive system, is in a particularly favorable position to assess the degree to which the institution has been able to support the teaching-learning effort—and if the support has been less than optimal, the reasons for the lowered level of support; the student has direct contact with his or her own behavior, with that of the

| Source | Target | | | | |
|---|---|---|---|---|---|
| | Student | | Instructor | | |
| | Academic Achievement | Learning Behavior | Teaching Behavior | Instructional Methodology | Institutional Support |
| Administrator | | | | | X |
| Student | | X | X | X | |
| Instructor | X | X | X | X | X |

**Figure 6.3.    Relations among Sources and Targets of Summative Evaluation**

instructor, and with the methodology used by the instructor in the instructional effort—and is hence in a favorable position to assess his or her own learning behavior, the teaching behavior of the instructor, and the methodology the instructor has used in the endeavor; and the instructor, having direct contact with all the targets of evaluation, is in a favorable position to assess each one.

## SUMMATIVE EVALUATION METHODOLOGY

The methodology available to the instructor for the summative evaluation of instruction is the same as that used in research in the social sciences and education. This methodology involves instrumentation, research design, data generation, data analysis, and frameworks for decision-making on the basis of evaluation findings.

While the methodology used in summative evaluation is common to students, instructor, institutional-support systems, and instructional procedures as evaluation targets, the following paragraphs will use examples of student-performance evaluation to discuss this methodology. The way it is used in the process of summative evaluation attending to the unique features of each target will be discussed later.

Two levels exist at which summative evaluation can take place: the individual level, in which the interest lies in the performance of a particular target; and the group level, in which the emphasis is on the use of inferential statistics to examine performance trends for students, administrators, or institutional-support systems. Research design and methods of data analysis at each of these two evaluation levels will be examined in turn in the following paragraphs.

## Instrumentation in Summative Evaluation

The types of instruments available to the instructor for the purpose of evaluation were discussed in Chapter 3. To summarize, they are *questioning instruments*, involving interviews, questionnaires, checklists and critical incident reports; *measurement instruments*, involving tests, projectives, inventories, sociograms and scaling techniques; and *observation instruments*.

Tests and critical-incident reports play central roles in summative evaluation, and they will be highlighted in the discussion that follows. The former are assessment instruments used to evaluate performance by reference to some set of criteria, and the latter are records of an individual's conduct under specific circumstances. The *Student Observation Record (SOR)*, the *Instructor-System Observation Record (ISOR)*, and the *Procedural Observation Record (POR)* shown in Figures 5.1, 5.2 and 5.3 respectively, are three critical-incident reports the instructor can use retrospectively for the purpose of summative evaluation.

## Data Generation Methodology in Summative Evaluation

There exist two principal ways in which the instructor can generate data in summative evaluation: *manipulatively* and *non-manipulatively*. The two approaches differ in terms of the control the instructor exerts over the processes examined. In the manipulative approach, the instructor takes some action (for example, delivery of a lecture) expected to bring about some outcome (for example, student learning). In the non-manipulative approach, the instructor allows whatever is assumed to bring about the result of interest to take place outside of his or her control and simply records the levels at which the events of interest occur. An example of non-manipulative data generation in summative evaluation is that of an investigator who collects information regarding student self-regulated learning and emotional functioning during instruction and then examines their impact on the students' mastery of the material. Assuming the instructor does nothing to influence the two former student attributes, the data-generation method involved would be considered non-manipulative.

The manipulative and non-manipulative approaches to data generation can be combined in one evaluative effort. For example, the instructor can implement an engagement module (manipulative data generation) and at the same time unobtrusively collect student self-regulation and emotional functioning information during engagement (non-manipulative data generation)—following which he or she can examine the way in which these student processes have impacted on the students' mastery of the material covered in instruction.

## Research Design in Summative Evaluation

As noted in Chapter 3, whenever he or she conducts research, it is important for the educator to control for possible confounding effects which may mislead him or her into concluding that something has caused something else to happen when that is in fact not true. This concern, involving internal validity (i.e., the degree to which an intervention and not extraneous factors is responsible for given outcomes), is as true of summative evaluation methodology as it is of any other research form. Often, a student's success in meeting instructional objectives is due to factors extraneous to the engagement effort. For example, private tutoring rather than the instructor's efforts can be responsible for a student's meeting some set of instructional objectives. In that case, it would be erroneous to conclude that the engagement effort has been successful— and, while the student's meeting of the objectives would be a cause for celebration, the same could not be said in this case for the effectiveness of instruction. In other cases, student success can be due to a combination of engagement and extraneous factors, and it may become difficult or impossible to ascertain how much was due to the instructional activities.

The two essential elements of research design in summative evaluation are the use of *pre-* and *post-tests*, and the use of *control* as well as *instructional* groups. A third element of research design in summative evaluation is often the randomized assignment of students to the different groups, which renders the design *experimental*. (When the instructor does not employ randomization, the research design is termed *quasi-experimental*.)

As noted in Chapter 3, one of the more sophisticated research designs available for the control of internal validity is termed the *pretest, posttest control group design* (*PPCGD*; Campbell & Stanley, 1963). This design, shown in Figure 6.4, enables the evaluator to control for pre-instruction performance and historical artifacts that may distort the effects of instruction in formative evaluation. As already noted, however, because the *PPCGD* requires the employment of both control and instruction groups, its use may not be feasible in many, if not most, instructional evaluation efforts – and the same holds true for the *Solomon pretest, posttest, multiple control group design* (*PPCGD*) that is best suited to control for test-retest effects. Nevertheless, it is important to re-emphasize that, particularly in the case of quasi-experimental studies, the degree to which the design for a given evaluation task approximates

|                          | Pre-Test | Instruction | Post-Test |
|--------------------------|----------|-------------|-----------|
| **Instruction Subject(s):** | $O_1$ | X | $O_2$ |
| **Control Subject(s):**     | $O_3$ |   | $O_4$ |

**Figure 6.4. Pretest, Posttest, Control Group Research Design**

those of these more complex schemes is the degree to which the evaluation findings can be considered credible. When randomization is limited, as it is in the typical instructional effort, the most restricted design possessing any degree of credibility is that shown in Figure 6.4, using single experimental and control groups. The use of this design will be assumed for the remainder of this discussion.

## Data Analysis in Summative Evaluation

The literature often distinguishes between two major forms of data analysis: *qualitative* and *quantitative*. In fact, the difference between the two approaches is not clear-cut, since the basis of all truly scientific quantitative analysis is qualitative, and a properly conducted qualitative analysis culminates with the quantitative processing of information. In fact, the best way to think about these two "forms" of analysis is in terms of a continuum ranging between qualitative and quantitative poles, and the question facing the researcher for any instructional evaluation effort is "Where in the continuum is the evaluation task facing him or her?" If the information at hand is purely qualitative in form (for example, written reports of student performance or completed written assignments such as those found in portfolios and performance records), the researcher has to begin at the extreme qualitative end of the continuum and work toward the quantitative end using the approach described next.

### Qualitative Analysis in Summative Evaluation

For either individual or group evaluation, if the information he or she collects is purely qualitative in nature, lacking any previously formulated methodology for content quantification and interpretation, then the instructor will have to devise some set of criteria for the interpretation and evaluation of the material. Knudson (1998) used the following method in a study which that author conducted to evaluate the essays of college-bound high school students:

1. Determine the criteria to be used for interpretation or evaluation of the work.
2. Test for expert consensus regarding the educational relevance of the criteria.
3. Develop a decision-making system for assigning a numerical value indicative of the degree to which the criteria are met.
4. Develop instructions for the use of the decision-making system.
5. Test the inter-judge reliability of the decision-making system.
6. Test the criterion validity of the evaluation scheme by correlating evaluation results with other previously validated measures of the same type of work.
7. Employ the criteria to assign a numerical value indicative of the judgment made concerning the quality or significance of the material at hand.
8. Process the quantitative information in the way described below.

The important point the instructor must keep in mind regarding this process of criteria development, quantification and validation is that he or she must follow it before undertaking the interpretation of qualitative information. Failure to do so is likely to yield evaluative information that is unreliable, invalid, or both.

## Quantitative Analysis in Summative Evaluation

If the information at hand for summative evaluation is in the form of numerical data such as test scores, scaled questionnaire responses, or ratings, the evaluator can begin at Step 8 above and use numerical analysis to process and interpret the information.

**Quantitative Analysis in the Summative Evaluation of Individual Performance**. When evaluating the performance of an individual subject, the instructor typically follows comparison of pre- and post-test scores with a determination of whether whatever difference emerges is large enough to be considered satisfactory. The criteria the instructor uses to make this determination are discussed below.

**Quantitative Analysis in the Summative Evaluation of Group Performance**. It was earlier noted that research design is intended to control for the *internal validity* of research findings. Now, there is also a need to control for the findings' *external validity*. This second concern with validity revolves around the question of whether instructional outcomes are due to the activities of the engagement effort or to chance—that is, whether repeated trials are likely to yield findings consistent with original outcomes. Inferential quantitative methods of data analysis exist to enable the investigator to address this question.

The more widely used inferential procedures available for group summative evaluation fall into three major categories: procedures for *the comparison of means*, procedures for *the test of correlations*, and procedures for *the comparison of proportions*. Procedures falling under these categories are discussed in Appendix A.

Thus, the methodology of summative evaluation involves the use of instruments, research design, and data-generation and analysis procedures. Although student examples were used above to illustrate the methodology of summative evaluation, these procedures can also be used in the summative evaluation of instructor and institutional-support performance. In fact, the procedures can be used for the evaluation of combinations of all the targets of evaluation. For example, an investigator can implement a university-wide program in which instructors, administrators and support staff are trained in modern principles of instruction. He or she can then evaluate the university's students, instructors, administrators and support staff following program completion to ascertain the program's effectiveness. In this case, the procedures involving instrumentation, research design, data generation, and data analysis described above would come into play for all of the targets of the evaluation effort.

While the methodology described above can apply to all targets of summative evaluation, each target has aspects unique to it that merit individual attention. The following paragraphs describe the process of summative evaluation for student, instructor, and institutional-support performance as well as for the effectiveness of the procedures used in instruction.

## THE PROCESS OF SUMMATIVE EVALUATION FOR THE VARIOUS EVALUATION TARGETS

### Summative Evaluation of Student Academic Performance

There are two aspects of student academic performance the instructor evaluates in the post-engagement phase of instruction: academic achievement and student learning behavior.

**Summative Evaluation of Student Academic Achievement**

Academic achievement involves the degree to which a student demonstrates mastery of the subject matter stipulated in instructional objectives at hand. As already noted, the instructor will be interested in evaluating the academic achievement of *individual students* as well as that of *groups of students*; in what follows, this feature of student summative assessment will be termed the *level* dimension of achievement evaluation. In addition, the instructor can take one of two approaches to evaluate student academic achievement: *criterion-referenced* testing and *norm-referenced* testing; in what follows, this feature of student summative assessment will be termed the *reference* dimension of achievement evaluation. While criterion-referenced testing involves the gauging of student test performance against instructional objectives, norm-referenced testing involves special statistical methodology for the gauging of student test performance against test performance by other students. As shown in Figure 6.5, the level and reference dimensions produce four testing contingencies possible in academic achievement evaluation. Each of these contingencies will be considered in turn for individual and group summative evaluation.

| Level | Reference | |
|---|---|---|
| | Criterion | Norm |
| Individual | | |
| Group | | |

**Figure 6.5. Testing Contingencies by Level and Reference in Summary Evaluation**

**Individual Student Summative Evaluation of Academic Achievement**. Individual student summative evaluation of academic achievement can be criterion-referenced or norm-referenced.

*Criterion-Referenced Testing in Individual Student Summative Evaluation*. In individual criterion-referenced summative evaluation, the difference between a student's pre- and post-test scores is compared against a criterion to determine the success of the teaching-learning effort. For example, assume that Bill, a college sophomore student, obtains a score of 70 on a post-test in calculus. Also assume that the instructional objectives for the engagement module stipulate a passing score of 65. Assume in addition that Bill scored substantially lower on a pre-test (say, 20), and that there is nothing other than the engagement activities occurred that may have influenced his post-test performance. Finally, assume that, as shown in Figure 6.6, pre- and post-test scores of

|  | **Pre-Test** | **Instruction** | **Post-Test** |
|---|---|---|---|
| **Instruction Student:** | 20 | X | 70 |
| **Control Student:** | 20 | | 20 |

**Figure 6.6. Evaluation Findings Using a Pre-Test, Post-Test, Single Student Control Research Design**

a student who did not receive the instruction shows no improvement. Given these findings, the instructor may be justified in concluding that the teaching-learning effort was successful in enabling Bill to meet the lesson's objectives.

*Norm-Referenced Testing in Individual Student Summative Evaluation.* In this form of evaluation, a student's test performance is typically interpreted as a percentile score derived from a table showing the proportion of students in a norm group (that group made up of the students against whom the performance is measured in norm-referenced testing) falling below his or her test score. For example, assume that Bill, the above student, obtains a score of 30 on a calculus test nationally normed with college sophomore students. A norm table may disclose that 84 percent of the students in the norm group scored below 30 on this test. In this case, Bill's percentile score is 84.

If no norm table exists for comparison but the mean and standard deviation of the norm group are available, the instructor can calculate a $z$-score (discussed in Appendix A) to determine the number of standard deviations above or below the norm-group mean that Bill's score lies. For example, if the norm-group mean is 28 and its standard deviation is 2, Bill's $z$-score, calculated as

$$z = (30 - 28)/2,$$

is 1. Bill's score thus lies 1 standard deviation above the norm group's mean. This value is the rough equivalent of the $84^{th}$ percentile.

Norm-referenced testing can be used to interpret a student's test performance relative to that of students in his or her own class as well as to that of students in an external group. A student's $z$-score calculated on the basis of the class' mean and standard deviation is typically used for the purpose.

Often, college administrators consider the findings of nationally norm-referenced evaluation useful for placement in competitive programs or for the awarding of honors and scholarships.

Regarding individual summative evaluation, it is important to keep in mind a potential limitation of the approach: since in the individual case an instructor can seldom know or control for all the extraneous factors that can influence an individual student's academic success, the condition raises some concerns regarding evaluation of the effectiveness of instruction in the case of individual student.

**Group Summative Evaluation of Student Academic Achievement.** As with individual student evaluation, summative evaluation of group academic achievement can take criterion- and norm-referenced forms. It was earlier stated that regardless of the form it takes, group summative evaluation requires the use of inferential statistics for its implementation. Through the use of inferential statistics, the investigator can determine whether evaluative findings are due to instruction or due to chance.

*Criterion-Referenced Testing in Group Summative Evaluation.* Group criterion-referenced testing involves a determination of whether on the average, a group of students has reached the instructional objectives stipulated for a given engagement effort. In this case, two questions arise as topics for investigation: first, what is the criterion for satisfactory work for any individual student in the group? Second, what will constitute a satisfactory proportion of the students meeting this criterion? The following is the process of criterion-referenced group summative evaluation:

1. Access of pre-test data for the experimental group(s), and if used, for the control group(s). (This data should have been generated earlier in the engagement phase of instruction.)

2. Administration of the post-tests to the experimental group, and if used, to the control group(s).

3. Reference to the research design in use to insure the appropriate choice of data-analysis procedure. As already noted, while the most sophisticated of the research designs available is that termed the Solomon

Pre-Test, Post-Test Multiple Group Design, it is seldom that conditions in the instructional setting allow for this complex scheme, and a compromise in the design such as that shown in Figure 6.4 is usually necessary.

4. Analysis of the pre- and post-test data for the control and experimental groups according to the specifications of the research design. Figure 6.7 shows a fictitious example of research outcomes comparing experimental and control group pre- and post-test means. Assume that the data relate to instructional objectives stipulating passing an end-of-course 40-point test with at least 65 percent accuracy.

|  | Pre-Test | Instruction | Post-Test |
|---|---|---|---|
| **Instruction Group:** | 10 | X | 30 |
| **Control Group:** | 10 |  | 14 |

**Figure 6.7. Fictitious Evaluation Findings Using a Pre-Test, Post-Test, Control Group Research Design**

In this table, while in the pre-test students in the experimental and control groups started with the same mean of 10 (25 percent accuracy for a test with a highest possible score of 40), on the post-test the experimental students scored with a mean of 30 (70 percent accuracy)—in comparison to the students in the control group, who scored with a mean of 14 (35 percent accuracy). Assume that in this hypothetical example statistical analysis shows that while the pre-test–post-test difference for the experimental group is statistically significant, that for the control group is not. Also assume that while the two groups did not differ statistically significantly on their pre-test scores, they do so on their post-test scores. Such outcomes would suggest that criterion-referenced gains for the experimental group are likely not due to such extraneous factors as test-retest effects, history, or chance, but to the activities carried out during engagement. The statistical procedure most widely used for this design is termed the repeated measures Analysis of Variance (ANOVA; this procedure is discussed in Appendix A).

5. Determination of the difference in the proportions of students in the control and experimental groups who met the passing criteria. Assume that 90 percent of the students in the instruction group obtained a score of 30 or higher and that 2 percent of those in the control group did so—and that the two proportions differ statistically significantly.

Given the above outcomes, the instructor has all the information he or she needs to decide a) whether the experimental-group students have met the objectives of instruction, and b) whether or not their success is due to the activities of the engagement effort. On the basis of the findings, he or she can conclude that the students in the instruction group have met the instructional objectives, and that the engagement interventions are responsible for this outcome.

***Norm-Referenced Testing in Group Summative Evaluation.*** Group norm-referenced testing is often used to determine school and instructor effectiveness by comparing student-group performance within a classroom or school with that of some other, usually larger, norm group.

For normed data, the instructor can use the same research design appearing in Figure 6.7 and the same statistical procedure described earlier for criterion-referenced group summative evaluations. He or she can use the design in one of two ways: first, he or she can form the control group himself or herself and then use pre- and post-test norm-based percentile or $z$-scores to carry out the control-experimental group comparisons. In the second approach, the investigator can forgo his or her formation of a control group and use the norm group as a kind of control against which to gauge the success of his or her students in mastering the material at hand. It is the second alternative that is typically involved when the term *norm-referenced testing* is used; it is the process of norm-referenced testing in this sense of the term that will be considered next.

The following is the procedure the instructor follows for norm-referenced summative evaluation of group academic achievement. He or she:

1.  Compares the instruction group's pre-test performance with that of the norm group through the use of percentile scores or $z$-scores.
2.  Administers the post-test to the instruction group.
3.  Determines the post-test percentile scores or z-scores of the members of the instruction group.
4.  Determines the difference between the pre- and post-test percentile or z-test scores.

As noted by Gabriel, Anderson, Benson, Gordon, Hill, Pfannestiel and Stonehill (1985), one potential limitation of norm-referenced testing in group summative evaluation has to do with the threats to internal validity encountered earlier. First, in the typical case, the instructor does not randomly assign students to the instruction group, rendering the design, at best, quasi-experimental in nature. Second, the instructor typically does not have access to norm-group pre- and post-test data *collected concurrently with that of the experimental group*— information in the absence of which he or she cannot control for historical threats to internal validity. These conditions can render norm-referenced summative evaluation findings uninterpretable or misleading. In fact, because the typical norm-referenced evaluation effort lacks this key information, the US Department of Education has discontinued the use of norm-referenced testing in the evaluation of any of a number of federally funded educational programs (Slavin, 1999). It should be emphasized that these reservations concerning norm-referenced testing do not hold when randomized, concurrently generated pre- and post-test information is available for both the norm and experimental groups.

Thus, the process of summative evaluation of student academic achievement involves the use of criterion-referenced as well as norm-referenced testing, and it can involve an individual student as well as groups of students. When groups of students are the targets of evaluation, inferential statistics are used to control for chance effects, and comparisons between control and experimental groups are used to control for threats to the internal validity of findings.

Often, a student fails to meet performance criteria stipulated in the instructional objectives at hand. When this occurs, the educator may want to ascertain the reason or reasons for the failure. To do so, he or she can examine deficits in student learning behavior during engagement that may have contributed to the problem. The matter of student learning behavior relative to academic achievement is considered next.

## Summative Evaluation of Student Learning Processes

The principal aspects of learning processes of interest in summative evaluation considered in the following paragraphs are the academic self-regulation, mental efficiency, emotional functioning, and management of multiple social roles that students bring to bear on their attempts to master material presented in the engagement phase of instruction.

**Academic Self-Regulation.** As noted in Chapter 2, academic self-regulation consists of motivation to do well in school, the realistic setting of academic goals, the use of effective strategies in pursuit of these goals, self-monitoring to gauge the effectiveness of the strategies used, and strategy adjustment as necessary. Lowered motivation and off-task behavior are opposite to academic self-regulation and are interpretable as deficits in this area.

The instructor can conduct a retrospective evaluation of student self-regulated learning behavior by reference to entries in the *Student Observation Record* (*SOR*, shown in Figure 5.1) related to self-regulation. The information the instructor seeks in this regard is whether the student manifested any deficits in self-regulation during engagement; and if so, the seriousness of the problem and the degree of success the instructor experienced in addressing it. An entry in the *SOR* showing that in the instructor's estimate a problem in this area was serious enough to interfere with learning but that it was not fully resolved during engagement points to it as a possible contributor to student failure to reach the objectives of instruction; it also suggests that the student will likely continue to experience the problem—and that in his or her case, remediation of academic self-regulation may be necessary before he or she can experience any success following further engagement activity addressing the objectives at hand.

**Mental Efficiency**. Mental efficiency, or ability, involves the speed with which a student has been able to acquire the information or skill conveyed during engagement, the effectiveness with which he or she has been able to retain and recall the information, and the extensiveness with which he or she can utilize it. As with academic self-regulation, the instructor can conduct a retrospective assessment of student mental acuity by reviewing the entries in the *SOR* related to this student attribute. The information the instructor seeks in this respect is whether the student manifested any problem in mental acuity during engagement; and if so, the seriousness of the problem and the degree of success the instructor experienced in addressing it. As before, an entry in the *SOR* showing that in the instructor's estimate the problem was serious enough to interfere with learning but that it was not fully resolved during engagement points to it as a possible contributor to failure to reach the instructional objectives; it also suggests that the student will likely continue to experience the problem—and that remediation of mental acuity may be necessary before the student can benefit from any additional engagement activity involving the objectives at hand.

**Emotional Functioning**. As with academic self-regulation and mental acuity, the instructor can review entries in the *SOR* for indications of emotional dysfunction manifested by the student during engagement. As before, an entry indicative of a serious, not fully resolved problem in this area during engagement is indicative that remediation of emotional functioning will likely be necessary before the student can benefit from similar instruction in any additional engagement activity involving the present instructional objectives.

**Management of Multiple Social Roles**. As before, the instructor can review entries in the *SOR* for indications of difficulties in the management of multiple social roles manifested by the student during engagement. An entry indicative of a serious, not fully resolved problem in this area during engagement is indicative that improvement in skills for multiple-social-role management will likely be necessary before the student can benefit from similar instruction in any additional engagement activity involving the present instructional objectives.

Thus, summative evaluation of student academic performance involves a determination of the degree to which students have benefited from instruction. In this respect, the interest lies in whether or not they have reached the instructional objectives (criterion-referenced summative evaluation), or in how their performance compares with that of other students (norm-referenced summative evaluation). In the case in which a student has failed to benefit from instruction, summative evaluation addresses the manner in which such student processes as self-regulatory, mental, and emotional functioning may have contributed to the problem.

In addition to assessing student academic performance, summative evaluation also examines the degree to which factors other than the student's behavior have contributed to his or her academic achievement. When a student fails to reach the instructional objectives at hand, this part of the post-engagement phase addresses the manner in which the instructor's performance, the quality of support provided by administrators and staff, or the effectiveness of the procedures used in the instructional process have contributed to the failure.

## Summative Evaluation of Instructor and Institutional-Support Performance

To evaluate his or her own performance as well as the support offered by the college's administration and staff during the recently completed engagement effort, the instructor can examine the *Instructor-System Observation Record (ISOR)*, shown in Figure 5.2, to review a) any problem encountered in these areas during engagement, b) the level of seriousness of the problem, and c) the degree to which the problem was resolved during the engagement phase. The *ISOR* makes provisions for recording critical incidents involving the instructor's own pedagogical skill and subject-matter expertise as well as the level of commitment he or she experienced during the engagement phase. The form also makes provisions for recording information regarding the quality of the support provided by the administration and school support staff during engagement.

An entry in the *ISOR* to the effect that in the instructor's judgment a problem encountered was serious enough to interfere with the success of the engagement effort but that it was not successfully addressed is indicative that the problem was not fully resolved—and that some sort of action will likely be necessary to improve the instructor's performance or the quality of school support before much more than before can be easily accomplished in any further engagement activity.

### Summative Evaluation of the Procedures Used in Instruction

To evaluate the procedures used in the instructional endeavor, the instructor can examine the *Procedural Observation Record (POR), shown in Figure 5.3*, to review any problem encountered with the design or execution of the needs assessment, diagnostic procedures, instructional objectives, task analysis, assessment methodology or engagement plan employed. The instructor can also review the *POR* to examine the seriousness of any problem encountered, and the degree to which the problem was resolved during instructional process.

An entry in the *POR* to the effect that in the instructor's judgment the problem was serious enough to interfere with the success of the instructional process but that it was not successfully addressed is indicative that the problem was not fully resolved—and that some sort of action will likely be necessary to insure the likelihood of success in future implementation of the instructional effort.

### SUMMARY

To recapitulate, summative evaluation involves a determination of the degree to which students have attained the objectives for a given instructional effort (a determination that constitutes the primary target of the evaluation); and, in cases in which they have failed to meet the objectives, the reasons for the failure (a determination that constitutes the secondary target of summative evaluation)—for example, the students' learning behavior, the instructor's performance, and the support lent to the teaching-learning effort by the institution.

As noted in Chapter 3, there are at least six major uses to which evaluation in instruction can be put: *instructional improvement, professional accountability and development, administrative supervision, examination of relations of student performance with classroom processes, protection of student interests*, and *awarding of merit pay*. As the term is used here, decision-making on the basis of summative evaluation outcomes refers to a determination of action to be taken to insure the success of subsequent instructional efforts involving the instructional objectives at hand. Remediation is one major decision possible on the basis of summative evaluation, and it is considered in the following chapter.

# Chapter 7

## Remediation

### INTRODUCTION

R emediation comes into play when problems identified through summative evaluation are judged serious enough to have interfered with learning—and to be likely to continue to do so unless resolved before any further attempts are made at addressing the instructional objectives at hand.

### THE PROCESS OF REMEDIATION

The process of remediation in instruction is similar in key respects to that of the teaching–learning effort described throughout this text; it involves, as a minimum, the following activities:

1.  Formulation of the objectives to be sought through the remedial effort
2.  Allocation of time and resources for the remedial effort

3.  Development of formative and summative evaluation criteria and methodology for the assessment of the success of the remedial effort
4.  Development of remedial interventions
5.  Execution and formative evaluation of the remedial interventions
6.  Summative evaluation of the remedial effort.

## REMEDIATION TARGETS

As already noted, there are four specific targets of remediation the instructor can identify in the post-engagement phase of instruction: the student's academic performance, the instructor's own performance, any of the procedures or activities of the three phases of instruction, and the support provided by school administrators and support staff. Regardless of the target, the remediation process always involves the six steps noted above.

### Student Remediation

In extreme cases involving student remediation, trained specialists such as college counselors and speech therapists may have to play leading roles in the planning and execution of the remedial effort.

Also, if in the judgment of those in the best position to decide, a student can be helped to overcome deficiencies identified through summative evaluation concurrently with work in the next juncture (lesson, course, level) in the student's program, then the remediation effort can proceed at the same time as work in the next juncture. Otherwise, the remediation effort may have to occur by itself, unaccompanied by work in the regular curriculum, before the student moves to the next phase in his or her program.

### Instructor Remediation

In the case in which the instructor perceives a need to improve his or her performance in instruction, he or she can seek to address the matter through one or more of several avenues available for the purpose. Callahan, Clark and Kellough (1998) listed a number of ways in which the instructor can seek to improve his or her teaching performance. One way is through *mentoring* or *peer coaching*, in which a) the instructor and mentor meet in a pre-observation conference and discuss the behavior to be observed, b) the mentor observes and coaches the instructor to help him or her to improve his or her performance, and c) the mentor observes the instructor once more and in a post-observation conference discusses the progress made and whatever work remains to be done. A second avenue the instructor can follow for self-improvement involves *in-service workshops* in which training and remedial work in specific areas are offered at the school or district level. A third avenue for instructor self-improvement involves *workshops and clinics* offered by professional organizations. Finally, the instructor can seek assistance in his or her self-remediation effort through *graduate study* through which he or she can keep abreast of the latest theory and research findings concerning the issues at hand.

## Methodological Adjustments

Methodological adjustments involve modifications the instructor makes in the procedures of the pre-engagement, engagement and post-engagement phases of instruction. There are three reasons for making such modifications. First, it is possible that, by reference to the *Procedural Observation Record* shown in Table 5.3 (see p. 109), difficulty in student academic achievement can be traced back to some procedure forming part of one of the three phases of instruction.

A second reason for such modifications is that theoretical and technological advances are constantly being made in virtually every aspect of the three phases of the instructional process, and procedural modifications are often necessary to keep up with such advances. Finally, even in the absence of external advances, the instructor's own thinking is likely to evolve concerning different aspects of the instructional process, and he or she may deem it appropriate to undertake the "fine-tuning" of these as his or her experience and thinking suggest.

## Institutional Support Remediation

When the instructor seeks to address deficiencies in the quality of support provided by administrators or support staff, the likelihood of his or her success increases if he or she approaches the problem *constructively*—that is, if he or she refrains from personalizing the problem ("What happened is your fault"), simply presenting the administrator or staff member with a complaint ("Things can't go on like this") or presenting him or her with an ultimatum ("Unless you change the way you do things, I'll complain to your superior")—and instead a) presents the problem objectively by referring to a common goal shared by the instructor and the administrator or staff member, and points to the problem as an obstacle to the common goal; b) shows the administrator or staff member how addressing the problem will benefit the institution as well as the student; c) proposes a number of attractive alternatives for the solution of the problem; and d) shows a willingness to work with the administrator or staff member to address the difficulty. It may be noted that the instructor can apply many of these same principles when he or she approaches a student with the task of embarking on remedial work to address some set of student academic deficiencies.

The preceding pages have discussed the matter of student, instructor, methodological remediation and school support in the face of student failure to reach some set of instructional objectives. In this respect, it is interesting to note that remediation may be necessary even though students successfully meet the objectives of instruction. Often, to achieve some set of educational goals, extraordinary efforts are necessary to overcome obstacles encountered in the course of engagement. But such efforts may not be possible in all future cases in which the same obstacles arise, and hence, prior to subsequent engagement activity, it may be necessary to take steps to prevent their recurrence. Thus, following engagement, remediation of some aspect of the instructional process may be required despite the fact that students have successfully met a lesson's instructional objectives.

## SUMMARY

To recapitulate, the post-engagement phase of college instruction examines the success of the activities of the instructional process, and the manner in which student, instructor, and institutional processes have contributed to or impeded the success of the teaching-learning effort. In addition, problems identified through summative evaluation can often be traced to any of the procedures comprising the three phases of instruction, rendering them targets for adjustment.

The success of the remedial activities of the post-engagement phase of instruction depends on the degree to which the evaluation effort meets a number of criteria: the instruments used for the collection and recording of information must be valid and reliable, the research design and data generation method used must insure the internal validity of the findings; and for group evaluation, the method of data-analysis must ensure the external validity of evaluation outcomes.

Finally, only through the feedback and self-adjustment afforded by the evaluative and remedial components of the post-engagement phase of instruction can the instructor continually improve the quality of his or her teaching efforts—and thus continually raise the likelihood that his or her efforts will significantly contribute to the academic success of his or her students.

# APPENDIX A

## Statistical and Research Concepts in College Instruction

### CLUSTER ANALYSIS

Cluster analysis (CA) is a statistical procedure used to ascertain the groups into which any number of individuals in a sample fall. The breakdown is performed on the basis of the distance between individuals on some measure. For example, after administering a questionnaire to assess attitudes toward gun control, a researcher can use the results to group the respondents according to how closely they score on the questionnaire. Two CA forms exist. The first, termed *hierarchical cluster analysis*, begins by grouping together the respondents who scored closest (i.e., those with the smallest difference between their scores), forming the first cluster; then, grouping with them those whose scores are closest to the original cluster's mean, forming the second cluster; and so on. The second, termed *k-means cluster analysis*, stipulating a set number of groups (for example, three), begins with the arbitrary calculation of three hypothetical group values and then the placing within each original group those individuals with scores closest to the group's mean; then, determining whether differences exist between the means of the new groups and the original means. The procedure continues until no differences emerge between the group means and subsequent means.

## FACTOR ANALYSIS

Factor analysis is a statistical procedure used to determine the common things, or factors, associated with a set of measures—and the degree of association between each measure and each factor. Typically, the analysis begins with a relatively large number of measures. On the basis of the correlations that emerge among them, the procedure tests whether they address a fewer number of factors. For example, for a test of anxiety containing 40 items, factor analysis may disclose that items 1–20, being highly correlated with one another, reflect a factor that can be characterized as *trait* anxiety; and that items 21–40, highly correlated with each other, reflect a factor that can be characterized as *state* anxiety. (Factors are named or characterized by ascertaining the things that highly correlated items share in common.) The test is said to possess convergent and discriminant validity if items 1–20 load exclusively on one factor and if items 21–40 load exclusively on the other.

In *exploratory* factor analysis, the researcher leaves it to the analysis to determine the number of factors involved and the degree of association of each measure with each factor. (The index of degree of association between a measure and a factor is termed a *factor loading*.) In *confirmatory* factor analysis, the researcher specifies in advance what he or she believes to be the factors and loadings at hand, and the analysis confirms or disconfirms these stipulations. According to Stevens (1996), loadings of .40 or above can be considered high enough to be empirically meaningful.

## GROUNDED THEORY RESEARCH

Grounded theory is a method of research through which the investigator begins with a minimum number of assumptions concerning the nature of the thing being investigated, letting the facts of the matter emerge in the course of his or her observations. Pressley and McCormick (1995) summarized this method in terms of the following steps:

1   Collection of qualitative data through observation or unstructured survey or interview methods
2.  Identification of regularities or categories among the qualitative data

3. Checking for category credibility and elaboration of categories through more focused observations, surveys, or interviews
4. Organization of categories into a cohesive theoretical structure
5. Construct validation of the theoretical structure through the use of statistical methodology.

Thus, grounded theory research combines the so-called qualitative and quantitative methods of research into one seamless process enabling the researcher to a) minimize his or her pre-conceived notions about the topic at hand, and b) use sophisticated mathematical methodology to examine the dynamics at hand with a degree of precision sufficient to afford explanation and prediction of the phenomenon at hand.

## INFERENTIAL STATISTICS IN GROUP SUMMATIVE EVALUATION

For any statistical procedure, a researcher may be interested in whether the findings for a particular sample can be generalized to the population from which the sample has been drawn. The branch of statistics addressing this question is termed *inferential statistics.*

The index used in inferential statistics to address this matter is termed the *p* value. A *p* value equal to or lower than .05 is interpreted as a low probability of being wrong if one accepts the hypothesis that the sample's findings can be generalized to the population. It should be noted that some controversy exists concerning the meaning of a *p* value. Martinez-Pons (1999) discusses this controversy in detail.

Three major classes of inferential procedures for group summative evaluation are *procedures for the comparison of means, procedures for the test of correlations,* and *procedures for the comparison of proportions.*

### Inferential Statistical Analysis for the Comparison of Means

Two major statistical-procedure families exist for the comparison of means: the Analysis of Variance (ANOVA) and *F*-test, and the *t*-test.

### The Analysis of Variance and *F*-Test

The Analysis of Variance (ANOVA) is the principal inferential statistical procedure used to examine differences between means. A variety of ANOVA models exist (see Hays, 1994, for an in-depth account of the different ANOVA models), of which one, termed the *mixed model*, is especially applicable for use in summative evaluation in instruction. This model is considered "mixed" because it enables the investigator to simultaneously examine differences *between individuals in different groups* as well as differences across time for *the individuals in the same group*. In this way, the procedure enables the investigator to analyze data in accordance with the research design appearing in Figure 6.7 (see p. 129). For example, to ascertain instructional effects, an instructor may have administered a maths test to a control group and to an instructional group before and after engagement. To determine whether the interventions have had their desired effect, the instructor can then perform a mixed-model ANOVA on the pre- and post-test data.

ANOVA yields two items of information: first, in what is termed an *omnibus* test, it shows whether an overall statistically significant difference exists between any two of the means involved, without specifying which means they are. Then, assuming a statistically significant omnibus outcome, through what are termed *post-hoc* pair-wise comparisons, the investigator contrasts the means two at a time to determine which pairs differ statistically significantly. In the above example, if, following a statistically significant omnibus outcome, *post-hoc* comparisons disclose a statistically significant gain for the instructional group but not for the control group, the instructor can probably conclude that the engagement activities have had their desired effect. When the researcher specifies in advance how he or she expects the means to differ, the pair-wise contrasts are termed *a priori* comparisons. An *F*-test is used in the Analysis of Variance to generate the *p*-value indicative of statistical significance.

In order for ANOVA to yield credible findings, the pre- and post-test data must be normally distributed; their variances must be equal; and the sample must be large, involving upward of 30 cases per group. When the data do not meet these requirements, the instructor may be able to use a less powerful (*power* in this case refers to the procedure's ability to detect statistical significance) but also less restrictive approach by ranking the data and then performing the ANOVA procedure with the rank values rather than with the original, raw data.

### The *t*-Test

A family of *t*-tests for means is often cited for possible application in summative evaluation in instruction. While the procedures involved have serious limitations for use in this capacity, their prevalence in educational research merits their discussion. Generically, the *t*-test is a statistical procedure used for the comparison of two means. When the means belong to two different groups, the researcher uses the *t-test for unrelated samples (TTUS)* to determine whether the groups differ statistically significantly. For example, an instructor can use the TTUS to determine whether a statistically significant difference exists in mathematics achievement between male and female students. The instructor can also use the TTUS when a) using one instructional and one control group and administering a post-test following instruction but no pre-test, as shown in Figure 4.10 (see p. 86); and b) assigning the students at random to the two groups. When the data do not meet the statistical assumptions of the TTUS (as with ANOVA, normal distribution; equal variances; and large sample, usually consisting of 30 or more cases) the investigator can use the Mann-Whitney *U*-test in its place. Although less powerful than the TTUS, the *U*-test is not subject to the relatively more restrictive assumptions of the TTUS.

When only one group is involved in the analysis and the investigator wants to test whether it differs across two time points on the same variable, he or she can use the *t-test for related samples (TTRS)* to perform the pre- post-test comparison. For example, he or she can use the TTRS to determine whether a statistically significant difference exists in a group of students in writing skills at the beginning and the end of the school year. The TTRS controls for possible confounding pre-test effects, thus enabling the instructor to more reliably gauge the effects of instruction on post-test outcomes than would be possible examining only post-test performance. When the data do not meet the assumptions of the TTRS (as with the TTUS, normal distribution; equal variances; and large sample, usually consisting of 30 or more cases), the investigator can use the *Wilcoxen z-test for two matched samples* to make the comparison.

The reader will note some important limitations in the *t*-tests for means for use in summative evaluation. On the one hand, the TTUS and its *U*-test counterpart do not control for test-retest effects; on the other, the TTRS and its *z*-test counterpart do not afford control-experimental group comparisons. But as already noted, particularly in the case of quasi-experimental designs, the essential elements of research design in summative evaluation are the comparison of experimental and control groups and the control for pre-test effects. These are requirements of summative evaluation that only the Analysis of Variance, described earlier in this chapter, can meet.

## Inferential Statistical Analysis for the Test of Correlations

Correlational analysis is a statistical procedure used to determine whether changes in one variable are accompanied by corresponding changes in another. For example, one may want to find out whether as a child grows older (change in age) he or she also grows taller (change in height). Three major classes of correlational analysis will be discussed in the following paragraphs: simple correlation, multiple regression, and path analysis.

### Simple Correlation

The most common index of correlation used today is the Pearson product moment coefficient of correlation, or Pearson correlation, signified by $r$ and ranging between −1 through 0 and +1. A positive (+) correlation means that as one variable increases the other also increases (for example, as children grow older, they tend to grow taller). A negative (−) correlation means that as one variable increases, the other decreases (for example, as children grow older, they tend to become less dependent on their parents).

Disregarding the sign, an $r$ between 0 and .20 can be considered low or weak, one between .21 and .40 can be considered moderate; one between .41 and .60 can be considered strong; and one between .61 and 1 can be considered very strong. As a general rule, $r$ is used when a sample size is equal to or greater than 30. With smaller samples, Spearman's rank correlation coefficient, or Spearman's Rho ($\rho$), is calculated by first ranking the values for the two variables and then calculating $r$ between the two ranks.

For $r$, a $t$-test produces a $p$-value indicative of statistical significance. A correlation of $r = .54$ with a $p$ value of .03 would show that for the sample at hand, increase in one variable is accompanied by a corresponding increase in the other—and that the finding can be generalized to the population with some degree of confidence.

### Multiple Regression

Multiple regression (MR; Martinez-Pons, 1999b) is a statistical procedure used to test the simultaneous correlation of one dependent variable with more independent variables than one. MR can be used to test for instructional effects while controlling for pre-test influences on post-test performance. To address the analysis requirements of the research design of Figure 6.7 (see p. 129), the model, termed a *multiple regression* model, can appear as in Figure A.1.

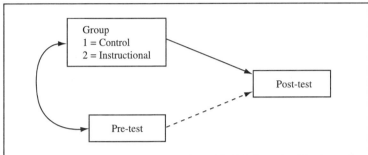

**Figure A.1. Multiple Regression Model for the Testing of Instructional Effects.** The dashed linkage represents the statistical control of pre-test effects on post-test performance. The curved linkage indicates a possible non-causal relation.

Multiple regression generates four major items of information. First, it generates a simple correlation ($r$) for each pair of linked variables. Second, it generates a regression weight (in standardized form, using $z$-scores rather than raw scores, represented by $\beta$), which shows the correlation between linked variable pairs while controlling for the confounding effects of other variables in the model. Third, it shows the *multiple correlation* ($R$) of a dependent variable with more independent variables than one. Finally, MR shows whether each of these items of information is statistically significant. To this end, it uses a $t$-test for $r$, a different kind of $t$-test for $\beta$, and $F$-test for $R$.

**Path Analysis**

Path analysis (PA) is a statistical procedure used to test correlation models containing intervening variables. PA enables the researcher to *decompose* the correlation between two variables into a) that which is spurious, inflated by the effects of other variables; b) that which is indirect, mediated by intervening variables, and c) that which is direct after all confounding and intervening effects have been accounted for. The procedure yields *path coefficients*, the same as the regression weights generated by multiple regression, which show the direct effects involved. It also yields *multiple correlation coefficients* ($R$), which show the degree to which a dependent variable simultaneously correlates with two or more independent variables in the model. Finally, the procedure enables the researcher to determine the most parsimonious form the model can take—that is, it enables the researcher to identify the simplest form the model can take to address the issues at hand. It does this through *model fitting*, which compares the power of the model for doing so with linkages excluded with all linkages included. One method widely used for the purpose of model fitting is termed the *comparative fit index* (*CFI* Bentler & Bonnett, 1980). A *CFI* greater than .90 is considered indicative of the justification in omitting given linkages to tell the simplest story possible in explaining the processes involved.

In the case of group summative evaluation, if he or she hypothesizes that a factor such as emotional functioning intervenes between self-regulation and academic achievement, the instructor may decide to use path analysis to test for such an effect. A hypothetical outcome of such an analysis might be as that shown in Figure A.2. In this figure, Pearson correlation coefficients appear within parentheses; and path coefficients, which show the direct correlation between variables while controlling for possible distorting effects of other variables in the model, appear without parentheses.

The fictitious outcomes appearing in Figure A.2 show an effect of engagement activities on academic achievement for the instructional group—even after academic self-regulation, emotional functioning and academic achievement pre-test performance have been statistically controlled. Of additional interest, the outcomes show that the effect of self-regulation on post-test scores has occurred partly through mediation of emotional functioning. The inferential information for $r$, $R$, and $\beta$ generated by path analysis is the same as that generated by multiple regression (see above).

### Path Analysis with Factors

Path analysis with factors (PF) is a statistical procedure used to test path models in which relations are stipulated among unobserved variables (i.e., factors composed of any number of elements). The procedure works in two phases. First, it performs what is essentially a confirmatory factor analysis for each factor stipulated in the model. Then, using these factors as single variables, the procedure performs a path analysis in the usual way. Single-measure variables as well as multiple-measure factors can be included in such an analysis. As in path analysis using single-measure variables exclusively, PF performs a test of the degree to which the model fits the data when not all possible linkages among variables and factors are stipulated. The *Comparative Fit Index (CFI)* is used to test the fit of the model. A *CFI* equal to or greater than .90 is indicative

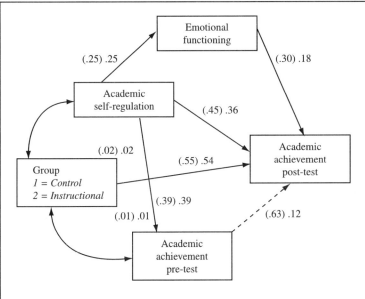

CFI = .99

Note: For each linkage, the Pearson correlation appears within parentheses, and the path coefficient appears without parentheses. The dashed linkage depicts the statistical control of pre-test effects. The curved linkages indicate possible non-causal relations.

**Figure A.2. Hypothetical Path Analysis Outcomes of the Effects of Instruction, Controlling for Self-Regulation, Emotional Functioning, Academic Achievement, and Pre-Test Scores**

of a good fit. PF models can include both factors and single-measure variables.

**Inferential Statistical Analysis for the Comparison of Proportions**

A $z$-test exists (Martinez-Pons, 1999b) that enables the instructor to determine the statistical significance of the difference between the proportions of students in a control and an experimental group meeting the performance criteria stipulated in a set of instructional objectives.

## THE MEAN, THE STANDARD DEVIATION, AND
## RELATED CONCEPTS

The mean ($M$) is the average of a set of scores; it is calculated by dividing the number of scores ($N$) into the sum of the scores, like this:

$$M = \text{Sum} / N$$

The standard (represented by $s$ for a sample or $\sigma$ for a population) is a measure of the differences that exist among a group of scores; it is calculated as a special average of the degree to which the scores differ from the group's mean. First, the square of the difference between each score and the mean is calculated, and then the square root of the mean of these squares is calculated, like this:

$$s = \sqrt{\frac{\Sigma(X - M)^2}{N}}$$

The symbol $\Sigma$ is an instruction to sum all squared differences between the scores and the mean. Without the square root, the value generated by the formula is termed the *variance*, represented by $s^2$ for a sample or $\sigma^2$ for a population.

$s$ is useful in a number of ways. For example, it can be used to estimate the effect of some intervention. In an instructional study by Orange (1999), $s$ for a control group was about twice as large as it was for an experimental group, showing that the intervention reduced differences among the members of the experimental group. Another way in which $s$ can be of use is in determining the degree to which a particular score differs from overall group performance. It can be used to this end by dividing it into the difference between the score and the mean to yield a *z-score*, like this:

$$z = (X - M) / SD$$

The *z*-score*z*-score provides an indication of the number of standard deviations above or below the mean a particular score lies.

## RELIABILITY

### Alternative-Forms Reliability

Alternative-forms reliability comes into play when the instructor plans to use two or more forms of the same test (for example, as pre- and post-tests for an instructional unit). Reliability in such cases involves the degree to which the alternative forms measure the same thing. The method used to assess alternative-forms reliability involves the correlation of scores for the different forms of the test. Depending on sample size, normality of distributions and measurement scales used, the statistical procedures used are Pearson's correlation coefficient, or *r*; or Spearman's *Rho*.

## Interjudge Reliability

Interjudge reliability involves the consistency with which two or more persons generate the same judgment on the bases of stated criteria or *rubrics*. For example, two observers may be given a number of criteria for judging the quality (*1 = poor, 2 = fair, 3 = good, 4 = very good* and *5 = excellent*) of an essay. Several methods exist of determining interjudge reliability. These methods can be classified according to number of judges and the scale of measurement involved.

The Goodman-Kruskall Lambda (Goodman & Kruskall, 1954) is used when a nominal measurement scale and two judges are involved. Scott's Pi (Withall, 1949) is used when the measurement scale is nominal and proportions are involved; Cohen's Kappa (Cohen, 1960) is used when raw frequencies for nominally measured variables are involved. Spearman's Rho or Kendall's *Tau* can be used when an ordinal measurement scale and two judges are involved. Kendall's coefficient of concordance is used when an ordinal measurement scale and three or more judges are involved, Pearson's correlation coefficient when an interval or ratio measurement scale and two judges are involved, and a special type of factor analysis termed Q-factor when an interval/ratio measurement scale and three or more judges are involved.

## Internal Consistency Reliability

The most common measure of internal consistency reliability, to which reference will be made later in this text, is Cronbach's *coefficient alpha* (*a*). This coefficient can range between 0 and 1. An *alpha* coefficient of 0 indicates that each item in the instrument addresses something totally unique to it, and a coefficient of 1 indicates that all the items in the instrument address exactly the same thing. In general, a coefficient equal to or greater than .70 indicates a high degree of consistency among the instrument's items.

## Test-Retest Reliability

Test-retest reliability involves the consistency with which an instrument assesses its target across time. It is measured by correlating responses to two administrations of the same instrument. For example, an attitude scale can be administered to 30 respondents twice, two weeks apart. Then, a Pearson correlation coefficient can be calculated between scores for the two administrations. A sufficiently high correlation coefficient (say, $r \Rightarrow .70$) would be interpreted as indicative that the scale assesses attitudes consistently across time.

# APPENDIX B

---

# The Alpha Method of Needs Assessment

## INTRODUCTION

The Alpha Method of needs assessment is designed to provide the college educator with a means for making key decisions concerning the content of instruction. The need for such an approach stems from the fact that the modern college instructor deciding what to include in his or her teaching endeavor is often faced with limitations in time and resources that influence his or her decision. In addition, in the modern college setting, a certain degree of compromise among instructor, students, and administrators is often required for any instructional endeavor to succeed. For these reasons, today's college instructor requires a method that enables him or her to identify those concerns that he or she can address through his or her instructional efforts, and to predict the level of support in the instructional endeavor that he or she can expect from key members of the college community.

The Alpha Method is based on the notion of *the stakeholder*, that is, any person, including the instructor, with an opinion concerning what the content of instruction should be—and with enough influence within the college setting to affect the viability of the instructional enterprise. Three distinct stakeholder groups involved in the typical college setting are students, administrators, and faculty members.

The importance of stakeholders in higher education is that, depending on their influence within the institution, stakeholders' support or resistance (budgetary backing or neglect by administrators; approval or disapproval by a faculty curriculum-review committee; course recommendation for or against, or participation in or avoidance by, students) can have great impact on the viability or success of an instructional undertaking—and such support can vary as a function of the degree of the stakeholders' satisfaction with instructional content. The calculations of the Alpha Method revolve for the most part around the concerns, influence, and level of support stakeholders are likely to present to the college instructional effort.

A key feature of the Alpha Method is the concept of *stakeholder press (SP)*, defined as the interaction between a person's *position (P)* regarding inclusion or exclusion of some topic in the teaching-learning effort; and his or her *influence (I)*, or capacity for affecting the viability or success of the instructional undertaking. The calculation of *SP* is described below.

A second key feature of the Alpha Method is the concept of *stakeholder thrust (ST)*, defined as the effective drive or support a stakeholder is likely to provide to the instructional effort given the content of instruction, the positive value the stakeholder has ascribed to parts of this content, and the influence that he or she can bring to bear on the viability or success of the instructional effort. The calculation of *ST* is described below.

A third key feature of the Alpha Method is the concept of *stakeholder resistance (SR)*, defined as the effective opposition a stakeholder is likely to present to the instructional effort, given the content of instruction, the negative value the stakeholder has ascribed to parts of this content, and the influence that he or she can bring to bear on the viability or success of the instructional effort. The calculation of *SR* is described below.

Stakeholder press, thrust, and resistance interact in such a way as to significantly impact on what the instructor includes in his or her teaching effort. The following pages describe the manner in which this influence is taken into account in the use of the Alpha Method.

## THE PHASES OF THE ALPHA METHOD

The Alpha Method is conducted in six phases: identification of stakeholders, identification of stakeholder concerns, calculation of stakeholder press, selection of stakeholder concerns to address through the instructional effort, determination of stakeholder thrust, and determination of stakeholder resistance.

## Identifying Stakeholders

As already noted, in the typical college setting there are three stakeholder groups with the capacity for influencing the viability and success of the instructional undertaking: administrators; faculty members, including the instructor; and students. Identification of administrators and faculty members as stakeholders can proceed on the basis of what the instructor knows about prospective participants' positions concerning the topic at hand. Of particular interest in this regard are administrators charged with time and resource (space, facilities, budgetary support) allocation, faculty members in curricular planning and review committees, and faculty members with expertise in the subject at hand. For the third stakeholder group, those scheduled to take the course at hand are the students most likely to have a stake in what the course entails, and hence, they can be identified by an examination of the course's student roster.

## Identifying Stakeholder Concerns

Stakeholder concerns involve opinions held by interested parties about what the content of instruction should be. The following steps are taken to identify the concerns of stakeholders through the Alpha Method (for the purpose of illustration, assume a college instructor using the method to conduct a needs assessment for a course in American history).

1. In an open-ended questionnaire or interview, elicit information about what stakeholders believe the course should cover. If a stakeholder is not available for questioning, estimate his or her answer on the basis of what is known about his or her position (public statements, private communication, official records). A review of official documents such as college-catalogue and college master-plan course descriptions can offer additional information about concerns regarding course content. The information is best gathered well before instruction begins in order to allow time for planning on the basis of the survey's outcomes.

In the present example, assume that the instructor conducts the needs assessment three weeks before the course begins. To this end, he prepares the following one-item open-ended questionnaire; "In your opinion, what topics should be included in course *H 102, American History*? Write down as many topics as you think should be included in this course." He distributes the questionnaire to the stakeholders and fills it out himself. In addition, he reviews the college-catalogue course description to identify possible topics for inclusion.

2. Analyze the information obtained through the open-ended survey and document review to identify major categories of concern. For the present fictitious example, assume that the instructor identifies nine concern categories expressed by the respondents or contained in the college-catalogue course description. These areas are shown in Figure B.1.

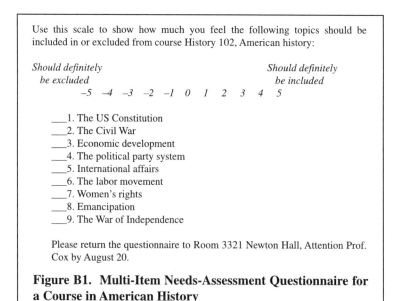

Use this scale to show how much you feel the following topics should be included in or excluded from course History 102, American history:

*Should definitely*                                          *Should definitely*
  *be excluded*                                              *be included*
                    –5   –4   –3   –2   –1   0   1   2   3   4   5

___1. The US Constitution
___2. The Civil War
___3. Economic development
___4. The political party system
___5. International affairs
___6. The labor movement
___7. Women's rights
___8. Emancipation
___9. The War of Independence

Please return the questionnaire to Room 3321 Newton Hall, Attention Prof. Cox by August 20.

**Figure B1.  Multi-Item Needs-Assessment Questionnaire for a Course in American History**

3. For each concern identified, develop a questionnaire item enabling a respondent to indicate his or her position about its inclusion in the instructional effort. The response scale can range between –5 (for definitive exclusion from the instructional effort) and 5 (for definitive inclusion). For the present example, the questionnaire the instructor develops might appear as that in Figure B1.

4. Administer the multi-item questionnaire. As before, the instructor may be able to estimate the answers a stakeholder not available for surveying might give on the basis of what is known about the stakeholder's position (public statements, private communication, official documents, etc.).

5. If two or more individuals in any stakeholder group have responded to the questionnaire, it is useful to perform a subject classification test such as a *k-means cluster analysis* to corroborate the stakeholder groupings the instructor has assumed. (See Appendix A for a discussion of cluster analysis; the end of Appendix B shows an SPSS/WIN syntax program with fictitious data for performing a cluster analysis for the present example.) If the analysis corroborates the original breakdown, then the rest of the calculations can proceed without further ado. If, on the other hand, the analysis disconfirms the original classification, an examination of the composition of each cluster will reveal the actual grouping. For the present fictitious example, the analysis outcomes corroborate the prior division of the respondents into administrators, instructors, and students. The rest of the analysis will be facilitated by use of the *Alpha Method Table (AMT)*, a matrix form developed for the purpose. For the present example, the *AMT* appears in Figure B.2.

6. Under each column of the *AMT* showing an area of concern, enter each group's questionnaire response mean at the top of the cell. In the present example, the entries are the means extracted through the cluster analysis shown at the end of Appendix B. For area 1, *US Constitution*, the response means are 2.75, 1.60, and 4.50 for administrators, faculty, and students, respectively; for area 2, *Civil War*, the response means are 2.75, 1.10, and 4.50 for administrators, instructors, and students, respectively; for area 3, *Economic Development*, the respective values are .75, −3.30, and 1.50.

## Ascertaining Stakeholder Press

Stakeholder press involves the pressure that a stakeholder can bring to bear on the educator to include or exclude given material in his or her instructional effort. It involves an interaction between the stakeholder's *position (P)* regarding inclusion or exclusion of some topic in the teaching-learning effort; and his or her *influence (I)*, or capacity for affecting the viability or success of the instructional undertaking. *SP* is predicated on the assumption that while a stakeholder's influence may be high, his or her desire that some topic be included in or excluded from the instructional effort may be low—and that while his or her influence my be low, his or her desire that some topic be included or excluded may be high—in either case limiting the press he or she brings to bear on the content of instruction. In the end, the interaction of *P* and *I* is likely to exert greater influence on instructional content than influence or position alone. This interaction is taken into account in the

**Areas of Concern**

| Group | Weight | 1 US Constitution | 2 Civil War | 3 Economic Development | 4 Political Party System | 5 International Affairs | 6 Labor Movement | 7 Women's Rights | 8 Emancipation | 9 War of Independence | Thrust Selected + Item Press Sum | Thrust % | Resistance Selected – Item Press Sum | Resistance % |
|---|---|---|---|---|---|---|---|---|---|---|---|---|---|---|
| Administrators | 3 | 2.75 / 8.25 | 2.75 / 8.25 | .75 / 2.25 | -3.00 / -9.00 | 2.00 / 6.00 | 4.25 / 12.75 | 4.50 / 13.50 | 4.50 / 13.50 | 4.25 / 12.75 | 29.25 | 22 | -9 | 7 |
| Faculty | 2 | 1.60 / 3.20 | 1.10 / 2.20 | -3.30 / -6.60 | 3.10 / 6.20 | 4.20 / 8.40 | 2.40 / 4.80 | 1.60 / 3.20 | 1.30 / 2.60 | .30 / .60 | 16.40 | 12 | 0 | 0 |
| Students | 1 | 4.50 / 4.50 | 4.50 / 4.50 | 1.50 / 1.50 | 2.25 / 2.25 | .50 / .50 | .25 / .25 | -2.00 / -2.00 | -4.50 / -4.50 | .00 / .00 | 11.50 | 9 | 0 | 0 |
| Total Press | | 15.95 | 14.95 | -2.85 | -0.55 | 14.90 | 17.80 | 14.70 | 11.60 | 13.35 | | | | |
| Total Press Ranking | | 2 | 3 | 9 | 8 | 4 | 1 | 5 | 7 | 6 | | | | |
| Time Required | | 10 | 15 | 10 | 3 | 10 | 10 | 15 | 15 | 1 | | | | |
| Resources Available | | 3 | 3 | 3 | 3 | 2 | 3 | 3 | 3 | 2 | | | | |

**Number of Items Selected:** 4

*HL:* 135

**Time Available:** 42 Hours

**Figure B2. Alpha Method Table.** Fictitious example of a needs assessment for a course in American History.

calculation of stakeholder press (SP), and hence, the latter is calculated as

$$SP = P \cdot I.$$

The following steps are taken to calculate stakeholder press:

1. Assign each stakeholder group a weight reflecting the influence its members can exert on the viability or success of the instructional effort. The weight scale can range between 1 for low and 3 for high. For each group, enter the weight under the *Influence Weight* column of the *AMT*. For the present example, assume that the instructor has assigned influence weights of 3, 2, and 1 to administrators, instructors, and students, respectively.

2. Multiply the group's questionnaire-response mean by the group's influence weight and enter the product in the corresponding cell underneath the group mean. In the present example, for *US Constitution*, these products are 8.25, 3.20, and 4.50 for administrators, instructors, and students, respectively; for *Civil War*, the respective responses are 8.25, 2.20, and 4.50; for *Economic Development*, the respective values are 2.25, −6.60, and 1.50.

## Selecting Stakeholder Concerns to Address Through the Instructional Effort

As noted earlier, resource and time limitations often restrict what the college educator can include in his or her instructional effort. In addition, conflicts between stakeholder concerns often make it necessary for the instructor to work out some form of compromise among the often conflicting desires for instructional content expressed by stakeholders. The Alpha Method uses the following steps to enable the instructor to select those concerns expressed by stakeholders to address through the instructional effort:

1. For each area of concern, add the parties' *Position × Influence* weight score products and enter the sum in the *Total Press* row. In the present example, the respective sums for *US Constitution, Civil War* and *Economic Development* are 15.95, 14.95, and −2.85.

2. Rank the sums of the areas of concern and enter the rank values in the *Ranking* row along the bottom of the *AMT*, with the lowest rank going to the highest product. In the present example, the ranking is, from left to right, 2, 3, 9, 8, 4, 1, 5, 7, 6.

3. Determine the time available (*TA*) for the course as hours per week × number of weeks. For a course meeting 3 hours per week in a

typical 14-week semester, $TA = 3 \times 14 \Rightarrow 42$ hours. Enter the $TA$ value in the lower right hand corner of the *AMT*.

4. Ascertain the availability of resources (space, equipment, materials, funding) to adequately cover each area of concern. A scale for the purpose can range between 1 (no resources available to adequately address the topic) through 2 (some resources available, but the adequacy of coverage is compromised) to 3 (all resources are available to adequately cover the topic). Enter the value at the bottom of the *AMT*, on the *Resources Available* row. In the present example, these entries are 3, 3, and 3 for *US Constitution, Civil War*, and *Economic Development*, respectively.

5. Determine the time in hours required ($TR$) to adequately cover each area of concern, and enter the value at the bottom of the *AMT*, on the *Time Required* row. In the present example, these time frames are 10, 15 and 10 hours for *US Constitution, Civil War*, and *Economic Development*, respectively.

6. Begin selection of topics starting with the lowest rank, keeping a running $TR$ total. Skip topics for which a 1 or 2 has been entered for resource availability.

7. Cease selection when the running $TR$ total exceeds $TA$. In the present example, for the first-, second-, third-, and eighth-ranking topics (*Labor Movement, US Constitution, Civil War*, and *Political Party System*, respectively), the resources are available for adequate coverage, and the combined time required does not exceed the total time available. Thus, the educator selects these four areas for inclusion in the instructional plan.

### Ascertaining Stakeholder Thrust

Stakeholder thrust is the drive, momentum or effective support a stakeholder is likely to lend to the instructional effort. The Alpha Method uses the following steps to estimate stakeholder thrust:

1. Calculate the highest possible stakeholder thrust level ($HL$) and record this value at the bottom right corner of the *AMT* for further reference. This value is calculated as follows:

$$HL = HW \cdot HV \cdot NI,$$

where

$HW$ = Maximum possible influence weight (in the present example, this value is 3)

$HV$ = Highest possible interest in inclusion of a topic in the instructional effort (in the present example, this value is 5)

$NI$ = Number of stakeholder concerns identified (in the present example, this value is 9).

In the present example,

$$HL = 3 \times 5 \times 9 \Rightarrow 135.$$

For each group:

2. Sum the stakeholder press *of the positively valenced areas selected for instruction*, and enter the total in the cell under the *Selected + Item Press Sum* heading. In the present example, these values are 28.25, 16.40, and 11.50 for administrators, instructors, and students, respectively.

3. Calculate *Stakeholder Thrust (ST)*. The calculation of *ST* is based on the reasoning that if a stakeholder group were to have the highest possible influence weight and were to assign the highest possible positive value to every topic identified (that is, if it were to exert the highest possible press), *ST* would equal *HL* and would thus constitute 100 percent of *HL*. Thus, *ST* is calculated as a percentage of the highest possible thrust, as follows:

$$ST = PS / HL \cdot 100,$$

where

$PS$ = the sum of the group's stakeholder positive press for the selected concerns.

Enter the value of *ST* for each group under the *Thrust* column of the *AMT*. For the present example, the values for the three groups are

$$ST_{administrators} = 29.25 / 135 \cdot 100 \Rightarrow 22.00\%$$
$$ST_{instructors} = 16.40 / 135 \cdot 100 \Rightarrow 12.00\%$$
$$ST_{students} = 11.50 / 135 \cdot 100 \Rightarrow 9.00\%$$

These values are interpreted as follows: The educator can expect that the administrators identified as stakeholders will lend 21 percent of their highest possible effective support to the content of the instructional undertaking. He or she can also expect that the faculty members identified as stakeholders will lend 12 percent of their highest possible effective support; and that the students taking the course will lend 9 percent of their highest possible effective support.

One way in which the instructor can address low thrust levels that emerge as happened in the present example is, assuming high levels of influence on the part of the parties involved, to attempt to persuade them of the importance of the areas on which they scored low on interest.

## Ascertaining Stakeholder Resistance

Stakeholder resistance (*SR*) is the effective opposition a stakeholder is likely to present to the instructional effort. The following steps are taken to estimate *SR*:

1. As before, calculate the highest possible stakeholder thrust level (*HL*) and record this value at the bottom right corner of the *AMT* for further reference. This value is calculated as follows:

$$HL = HW \cdot HV \cdot NI$$

where

*HW* = Maximum possible influence weight (in the present example, this value is 3)

*HV* = Highest possible interest in inclusion of a topic in the instructional effort (in the present example, this value is 5)

*NI* = Number of stakeholder concerns identified (in the present example, this value is 9).

In the present example,

$$HL = 3 \times 5 \times 9 \Rightarrow 135.$$

For each group:

2. Sum the stakeholder press *of the negatively valenced areas selected for instruction* and enter the total in the cell under the *Selected – Item Press Sum* heading. In the present example, these values are –9, 0, and 0 for administrators, instructors, and students, respectively.

3. Calculate *Stakeholder Resistance* (*SR*). The calculation of *SR* is based on the reasoning that if a stakeholder group were to have the highest possible influence weight and were to assign the highest possible negative value to every topic identified (that is, if it were to exert the highest possible negative press), *SR* would equal negative *HL* and would thus constitute 100 percent of negative *HL*. Thus, *SR* is calculated as a percentage of the highest possible resistance, as follows:

$$SR = NS / HL \cdot 100$$

where

$NS$ = the sum of the group's stakeholder negative press for the selected concerns.

Enter the value of $SR$ for each group under the *Resistance* column of the *AMT*. For the present example, the values for the three groups are

$$SR_{administrators} = -9 / -135 \cdot 100 \Rightarrow 7.00\%$$
$$SR_{instructors} = 0 / -135 \cdot 100 \Rightarrow 0.00\%$$
$$SR_{students} = 0 / -135 \cdot 100 \Rightarrow 0.00\%$$

These values are interpreted as follows:

Given the content of the present instructional plan, the educator can expect that the administrators identified as stakeholders will present 9 percent of their highest possible resistance to the undertaking. He or she can also expect no resistance from faculty members identified as stakeholders or students taking the course.

There are ways in which the instructor can address projected stakeholder resistance to his or her instructional undertaking: first, he or she can attempt to change the opposing party's stance by correcting any misconception that may underlie the opposition. For example, at the university where the present author teaches, a professor had a proposal he submitted for a psychology course rejected by a curriculum review committee when the reviewers noticed the term *parapsychology* in the course's title and assumed that the proposal involved a course on the occult. The professor was able to change the reviewers' minds by explaining that the course was designed to enable students to be critical of unfounded claims made by proponents of parapsychological phenomena—and in this way to help sharpen students' scientific thinking skills. Following his explanation, the committee reversed its decision and approved the course.

A second way in which the instructor can address projected stakeholder resistance to his or her instructional undertaking is to modify the course description to emphasize favored components and de-emphasize elements the stakeholders find objectionable.

A third way in which the instructor can address projected stakeholder resistance to the instructional undertaking is to simply eliminate elements to which the stakeholders strongly object.

A fourth way in which the instructor can address projected stakeholder resistance is to seek some sort of compromise by offering to address course material the stakeholders would favor along with that to which they object. This approach often works well when the instructor points to the need to strike a balance between divergent views and to thus insure objectivity in the approach to the subject matter.

In summary, the Alpha Method is designed to enable the college instructor to attend to demands placed on the instructional effort by stakeholders, that is, by individuals in a position to influence the viability of the teaching-learning effort. The objectives in using the Alpha Method are, given stakeholder conflict and resource limitations, to select the optimal content of instruction; and then, having decided on the content of instruction, to determine the likely support or resistance to expect from stakeholders.

## SPSS/WIN CLUSTER ANALYSIS SYNTAX PROGRAM
## FOR USE WITH THE ALPHA METHOD

```
DATA LIST   FREEFIELD RECORDS = 1
/ 1 A1 TO A9 WEIGHT GROUP  ID.

COMPUTE TOT=SUM (A1 TO A9).

VALUE LABELS GROUP 1 'ADMINISTRATORS' 2 'STUDENT'
3 'INSTRUCTORS'.

BEGIN DATA.
5   4   1   3   0   0  -1  -5   0   3   1   01
4   5   2   2   1   1  -2  -4   0   3   1   02
5   4   1   1   0   0  -3  -5   0   3   1   03
4   5   2   3   1   0  -2  -4   0   3   1   04
2   0  -3   2   4   1   2   1   0   2   2   05
1   1  -2   3   5   2   1   1   0   2   2   06
2   1  -3   2   3   2   1   1   0   2   2   07
2   1  -4   4   3   3   2   2   1   2   2   08
2   1  -3   3   4   3   2   2   0   2   2   09
1   2  -4   3   5   3   2   1   0   2   2   10
1   1  -4   3   4   3   1   2   1   2   2   11
1   1  -3   3   5   2   1   1   0   2   2   12
2   2  -4   4   5   2   2   1   1   2   2   13
2   1  -3   4   4   3   2   1   0   2   2   14
3   3   0  -2   2   5   5   4   4   1   3   15
3   3   0  -3   2   4   4   5   4   1   3   16
3   3   1  -4   2   4   5   4   4   1   3   17
2   2   2  -3   2   4   4   5   5   1   3   18
END DATA.

QUICK CLUSTER A1 TO A9
/CRITERIA CLUSTER (3)
/ PRINT CLUSTER ID (GROUP).
```

## CLUSTER ANALYSIS OUTCOMES FOR THE USE OF
## THE ALPHA METHOD

```
* * * * * * * * * * * * QUICK CLUSTER * * * * * * * * * * * *
Convergence achieved due to no or small distance change.
The maximum distance by which any center has changed is
.0000. Current iteration is 3 Minimum distance between
initial centers is 7.0711
```

Minimum distance between initial centers is 10.5830

| Iteration | Change in Cluster Centers | | |
|---|---|---|---|
| | 1 | 2 | 3 |
| 1 | 1.9526 | 2.22382 | 1.9685 |
| 2 | .0000 | .0000 | .0000 |

Case listing of Cluster membership.

| GROUP | Cluster | Distance |
|---|---|---|
| 3.00 | 3 | 1.696 |
| 3.00 | 3 | 1.369 |
| 3.00 | 3 | 1.969 |
| 3.00 | 3 | 1.369 |
| 2.00 | 2 | 2.238 |
| 2.00 | 2 | 1.847 |
| 2.00 | 2 | 1.900 |
| 2.00 | 2 | 2.100 |
| 2.00 | 2 | 1.187 |
| 2.00 | 2 | 1.735 |
| 2.00 | 2 | 1.616 |
| 2.00 | 2 | 1.345 |
| 2.00 | 2 | 1.952 |
| 2.00 | 2 | 1.345 |
| 1.00 | 1 | 1.677 |
| 1.00 | 1 | 1.146 |
| 1.00 | 1 | 1.346 |
| 1.00 | 1 | 1.953 |

\* \* \* \* \* \* \* \* \* \* \* QUICK CLUSTER (Cont.) \* \* \* \* \* \* \* \* \* \* \*

Final Cluster Centers.

| Cluster | A1 | A2 | A3 | A4 |
|---|---|---|---|---|
| 1 | 2.7500 | 2.7500 | .7500 | −3.0000 |
| 2 | 1.6000 | 1.1000 | −3.3000 | 3.1000 |
| 3 | 4.5000 | 4.5000 | 1.5000 | 2.2500 |

| Cluster | A5 | A6 | A7 | A8 |
|---|---|---|---|---|
| 1 | 2.0000 | 4.2500 | 4.5000 | 4.5000 |
| 2 | 4.2000 | 2.4000 | 1.6000 | 1.3000 |
| 3 | .5000 | .2500 | −2.0000 | −4.5000 |

| Cluster | A9 |
|---|---|
| 1 | 4.2500 |
| 2 | .3000 |
| 3 | .0000 |

- - - - - - - - - - - - - - - - - - - - - - - - - - - - - - - - - - - - - -

Number of Cases in each Cluster.

| Cluster | Unweighted cases | Weighted cases |
|---|---|---|
| 1 | 4.0 | 4.0 |
| 2 | 10.0 | 10.0 |
| 3 | 4.0 | 4.0 |
| Missing | 0 | |
| Valid cases | 18.0 | 18.0 |

- - - - - - - - - - - - - - - - - - - - - - - - - - - - - - - - - - - - - -

# APPENDIX C

## The Activities of the Instructor-Student Dialogue and Course Project

### AGREEING ON A TOPIC FOR INQUIRY

The first task in the conduct of the dialogue is to select a topic for exploration. The topic should meet the following criteria:

1. It should be selected by the student.
2. It should be part of the material covered in the course.
3. It should be one the student has not fully explored in the past.
4. It should be one that can be adequately addressed in the time allotted for the course.
5. It should be one in which the instructor has some expertise or one in which the instructor can acquire the expertise in preparation for the dialogue.

To prepare for this task, the instructor and student review the issue-oriented literature, that is, the literature suggesting that the topic merits study. For the purpose of illustration, assume that, on the basis of their review of the issue-oriented literature, a student and his or her instructor agree on *family child abuse* as the topic for study for the course project.

## FOCUSING THE TOPIC

*Focusing the topic* refers to a decision concerning that aspect of the topic at hand which is to be explored through the dialogue and course project. There are five principal ways in which a topic can be focused for investigation (Martinez-Pons, 1997): the first, termed the *construct descriptive focus*, involves the delineation of some construct or concept in such a way as to render it observable and measurable. As an example of modern inquiry conducted through the construct descriptive focus, Salovey and Mayer (1989) developed a descriptive model of *emotional intelligence* as a three-component construct: attention to, and differentiation and regulation of, one's moods and emotions.

The second way in which a topic for modern inquiry can be focused is through the *development of methodology for the assessment or information-gathering methodology regarding some previously delineated construct*. As an example of inquiry carried out through the assessment focus, Salovey, Mayer, Goldman, Turvey and Palfai (1995) developed the *Trait Meta-Mood Scale* for the assessment of emotional intelligence.

The third way in which a topic for modern inquiry can be focused is through the *analysis and interpretation of demographic data*. As an example of modern inquiry carried out through the demographic focus, the US Census Bureau regularly conducts national surveys of indices of living standards.

The fourth way in which a topic for modern inquiry can be conducted is through the *historical focus*, that is, through the study of *occurrences leading to landmark social events and practices*; or events *leading to the formation, growth and decline of distinct social systems or institutions*. As examples of inquiry carried out through the historical focus, the student may want to study the history of the practice of mental testing in the United States, or to study the social movement that led to the creation of public education in the United States.

The fifth focus in modern inquiry involves the *determination of the causes and effects* of reoccurring social or psychological processes. As an example of research carried out through the causal focus, the student may want to study the reasons some parents abuse third children, and the effects of child abuse on children's social development. Martinez-Pons (1997b) describes in detail the five ways of focusing a topic for inquiry.

In determining which focus to use, the instructor and student review the theory- and research-oriented literature to determine whether work exists that can serve as foundation for the work at hand. For the present example, assume that, on the basis of his or her theory-oriented literature, the student decides that enough construct descriptive and assessment methodology work has been done to make possible the use of the causal focus for this topic—and that hence he or she decides to use the causal focus for his or her investigation.

## DEVELOPING A CONCEPTUAL FRAMEWORK OR MODEL TO GUIDE THE INQUIRY

There are several forms of activity the instructor and student can perform to develop the model for investigation. First, they can conduct observations to try to gain a sense of the nature of the phenomenon in question. Second, they can *brainstorm* to hypothesize about the nature of the phenomenon. Third, they can review the literature to determine what others have said regarding the nature of the thing in question.

Assume for the present example that the student has found works in the theory-oriented literature arguing or speculating that *child abuse* has a negative influence on the child's *level of social interaction* and *social development*; and that the *level of social interaction* has an effect on the child's *social development*. Also assume that the theory-oriented literature suggests that *socio-economic status* influences *child abuse* and *social development*. Assume that on the basis of these findings the student develops the causal model appearing in Figure C.1. Note that the linkages in this model are numbered; the student will use these numbers later when he or she develops the research questions and hypotheses.

## ASSESSING THE MODEL'S STRUCTURAL INTEGRITY

A model's structural integrity consists of *differentiation*, or the matter of whether the different parts of the model are indeed different from each other rather than synonyms of each other; *cohesiveness*, or the matter of whether the relations stipulated among the different parts of the model make intuitive sense—for example, a historical model in which Lincoln's assassination is hypothesized to have led to the US Civil War would lack cohesiveness because the assassination occurred following the end of the war; and *comprehensiveness*, or the matter of whether the model contains enough detail to fully address the issue at hand.

The model overleaf would appear to meet the *differentiation* and *cohesiveness* criteria of structural integrity, although other variables such as *the parent having been abused as a child* and *family isolation* would probably add significantly more information to that offered by the

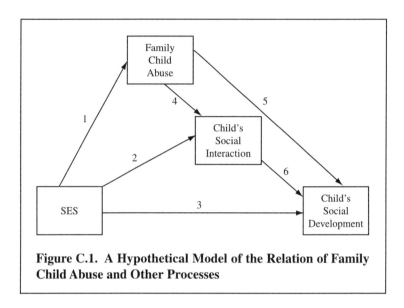

**Figure C.1. A Hypothetical Model of the Relation of Family Child Abuse and Other Processes**

present model (for the purpose of illustration, the number of variables included was limited to four).

## TESTING THE MODEL'S INSTRUMENTAL STRENGTH

*Instrumental strength* refers to the matter of whether each component of the model can be conceptualized or described in such a way as to render it observable and unambiguous. For the present example, *SES* can be defined as a composite of the parents' educational level, annual salary, and occupation; *child abuse* can be defined as punishment that is either unwarranted, consistently ineffective, or permanently damaging to the child; *social interaction* can be defined as *the frequency, duration and intensity with which the child interacts with other children*; and *social development* can be defined as *cooperative, supportive and self-assertiveness skills*.

## PREPARING TO TEST THE MODEL'S
## EMPIRICAL VALIDITY

Before the model can be tested for empirical validity, the instructor and student must develop a set of research questions and hypotheses that will guide the validation effort.

## Developing the Research Questions

Development of the research questions for the present study involves the verbalization of linkages in the hypothetical model in question format, with as many research questions as there are linkages. For the present example, there are six research questions which the student would verbalize as follows:

1. Is there a relation between *SES* and *family child abuse?*
2. Is there a relation between *SES* and *social interaction?*
3. Is there a relation between *SES* and *social development?*
4. Is there a relation between *family child abuse* and *social interaction?*
5. Is there a relation between *family child abuse* and *social development?*
6. Is there a relation between *social interaction* and *social development?*

## Developing Hypotheses

Hypotheses are tentative answers to research questions. To generate these tentative answers, the instructor and student review the research-oriented literature. For the present example, their review of the research-oriented literature might lead the student to develop the following hypotheses:

1. A negative relation exists between *SES* and *child abuse* (i.e., as *SES* increases, *family child abuse* decreases).
2. A positive relation exists between *SES* and *social interaction* (i.e., as *SES* increases, the child's level of *social interaction* increases).
3. A positive relation exists between *SES* and *social development* (i.e., as *SES* increases, social development increases).
4. A negative relation exists between *family child abuse* and the child's level of *social interaction* (i.e., as child abuse increases, social interaction decreases).
5. A negative relation exists between *family child abuse* and the child's *social development* (i.e., as child abuse increases, social development decreases).

## TESTING THE MODEL'S EMPIRICAL VALIDITY

The test of a model's empirical validity entails the use of sampling methodology, research design, instrumentation, data-generation methodology, data analysis, and systems for decision-making relative to research findings.

Assume that for the present example the student uses a sample of 300 families selected at random in a large metropolitan area for the study, that he or she uses the research design appearing in Figure C.3 calling for the statistical control of intervening and confounding effects, that he or she uses questionnaires as the information-gathering instruments, a survey as the data-generation method, and path analysis as the method of data analysis. Also assume that the student decides to use correlations at or above .10 as indicative of a meaningful relationship and a statistical significance level of .05 (see Appendix A for discussions of correlation and statistical significance) as supportive of the hypotheses.

Also assume that the path analysis yields the following fictitious information:

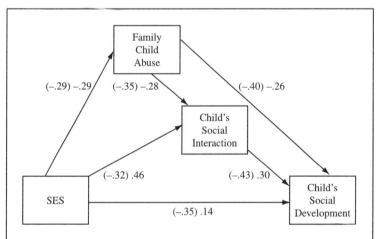

Note: The fictitious Pearson correlation coefficients appear within parentheses, and the path coefficients appear without parentheses. All coefficients are statistically significant beyond the .05 level.

**Figure C.2.   Path Analysis Outcomes of Fictitious Child Abuse Data.**

## DRAWING CONCLUSIONS ON THE BASIS OF THE OUTCOMES OF THE INVESTIGATION

Drawing conclusions involves deciding whether the results of the data analysis have supported or disconfirmed the hypotheses developed for investigation, given the decision-making criteria the investigator has stipulated in advance.

For the present example, the student can conclude that all his or her hypotheses have been supported, although in more complex ways than might have been expected had each linkage been examined independently. For example, although the correlation of *SES* with *social development* was $r = .35$, it decreased to $\beta = .14$ when the intervening effects of *child abuse* and *social interaction* were statistically controlled— meaning that about half of the effect of *SES* on *social development* was indirect.

## ON THE BASIS OF THE CONCLUSIONS, DECIDING ON WHAT THE NEXT TOPIC FOR CONSIDERATION SHOULD BE

On the basis of the conclusions, the investigator suggests topics for further study and, possibly, makes recommendations for policy-making. In the present example, the student may want to suggest that, given the limited level of comprehensiveness of the model, further study be conducted including other variables such as *the parent having been abused as a child* and *family isolation*. In addition, given findings such as those in the present fictitious study, the student might want to make recommendations concerning ways in which families can be educated regarding the negative effect of child abuse on their offspring's social development, and regarding ways in which such abuse can be minimized.

## PREPARING THE PROJECT REPORT

Following completion of the process of the course project, the student prepares a report describing the activities and findings of the study. A format of this report was shown in Chapter 4 (see pp. 49–92) and is repeated in Figure C3.

**Title**

**Author**

**Introduction**

The Issue
Limitations in the Way the Issue Has Been Addressed Up to Now
Purpose
Reasons for the Study
Broad Perspective of the Present Effort
        General Theoretical Framework
        The Study's Hypothetical Model
Research Questions and Hypotheses

**Method**

Sample
Research Design
Instrumentation
Data Generation Procedure
Method of Data Analysis

**Results**

Data Analysis Outcomes
Interpretation of Analysis Outcomes Relative to the Hypotheses

**Discussion**

Reiteration of the Purpose of Study and the Hypotheses
Significance of the Support or Non-Support of the Hypotheses
Implications for Theory and Practice
Limitations of the Study and Recommendations for Further Research

**References**

**Figure C3.  General Outline for the Project Report**

# APPENDIX D

## Self-Regulation Scale of Emotional Intelligence (SRSEI)

(From Martinez-Pons, 2000a)

**Use this scale to show how much you agree with each of the following statements:**

*completely disagree*       *completely agree*
     1     2     3     4     5     6     7

__1. I can maintain better control of my life if I keep in touch with my moods and emotions.

__2. I am able to overcome any distractions that arise as I try to keep in touch with my moods and emotions.

__3. I find it worthwhile to spend the time and effort necessary to keep in touch with my moods and emotions.

__4. I am able to maintain better control of my life if I am able to sort out my moods and emotions.

__5. I am able to overcome any obstacles that arise as I try to sort out my moods and emotions.

__6. I find it worthwhile to spend the time and effort necessary to sort out my moods and emotions.

__7. I can maintain better control of my life if I can effectively manage my moods and emotions.

__8. I am able to overcome any obstacles that arise as I try to manage my moods and emotions.

__9. I find it worthwhile to spend the time and effort necessary to manage my moods and emotions.

**How often do you try to reach or maintain the following goals relative to being in touch with your moods and emotions? Use this scale to show your responses:**

*I never try to reach*          *I'm always trying to reach*
*or maintain this goal*         *or maintain this goal*
       1      2      3      4      5      6      7

__10. in general, to be in touch with your moods and emotions
__11. to know how you are feeling at any point in time
__12. to be aware when you are switching between one emotion and another
__13. to be able to tell how your behavior is being affected by your emotions
__14. to be able to tell *how strongly* you feel about something
__15. to keep a daily record of your moods and emotions.

**How often do you take the following steps in trying to keep in touch with your moods and emotions? Use this scale to show your responses:**

                                *I'm always doing this*
                                *(this is part of*
*I never do this at all*          *my daily routine)*
       1      2      3      4      5      6      7

__16. taking "time out" to reflect about how you are feeling
__17. asking yourself, "how am I feeling now?"
__18. ascertaining your feelings by noting your heartbeat, breathing and other bodily processes
__19. avoiding the suppression or "squelching" of your moods and emotions
_ 20. being on the alert for early signs of emotional distress
__21. ascertaining your feelings by noting how you are behaving
__22. observing others' reactions to your behavior to determine how your moods and emotions are affecting you
__23. keeping a written record of daily changes in your moods and emotions.

**How often do you try to reach or maintain the following goals in sorting out your moods and emotions? Use this scale to show your responses:**

                                *I'm always doing this*
                                *(this is part of*
*I never do this at all*          *my daily routine)*
       1      2      3      4      5      6      7

__24. in general, to sort out the various moods and emotions you are experiencing at any given time
__25. to be able to tell the number of moods and emotions you are experiencing
__26. to tell how the moods and emotions you are experiencing differ from each other
__27. to determine the strength of each mood or emotion you are experiencing
__28. to determine how your different moods and emotions interact to affect your general state of mind.

**How often do you take the following steps in trying to sort out your moods and emotions? Use this scale to show your responses:**

                                *I'm always doing this*
                                *(this is part of*
*I never do this at all*          *my daily routine)*
       1      2      3      4      5      6      7

__29. developing a clear idea of the range of moods and emotions you are capable of experiencing

__30. naming the different moods and emotions you are experiencing at any given time

__31. noting what action the different moods or emotions seems to elicit on your part

__32. noting what happens just before you begin experiencing each mood or emotion

__33. noting what is happening during the time that you are experiencing each mood or emotion

__34. noting how each mood or emotion is affecting your ability to think clearly

__35. noting how each mood or emotion is affecting your ability to complete a task.

**How often do you try to reach or maintain the following goals relative to your moods or emotions? Use this scale to show your responses:**

|  | | *I'm always doing this* |
|---|---|---|
| | | *(this is part of* |
| *I never do this at all* | | *my daily routine)* |
| 1 | 2 | 3 | 4 | 5 | 6 | 7 |

__36. in general, to effectively manage your moods and emotions

__37. to increase or decrease the strength of a mood or emotion to enable you to regain or maintain your "peace of mind"

__38. to increase or decrease the strength of the mood or emotion to enable you to more efficiently perform a task

__39. to stop a negative mood or emotion from worsening to enable you to maintain or regain "peace of mind"

__40. to stop a negative mood or emotion from worsening in order to arrest deterioration of your performance on some task

__41. to compensate for the negative effect of some mood or emotion to enable you to regain your "peace of mind"

__42. to compensate for the negative effect of some mood or emotion in order to enable you to perform some task

__43. to use information from a daily record of your moods and emotions to plan future activities.

**How often do you use the following strategies in trying to manage your moods and emotions? Use this scale to show your responses:**

|  | | *I'm always doing this* |
|---|---|---|
| | | *(this is part of* |
| *I never do this at all* | | *my daily routine)* |
| 1 | 2 | 3 | 4 | 5 | 6 | 7 |

__44. challenging the thought precipitating a negative mood or emotion (e.g., reinterpreting a negative situation "to see its bright side")

__45. modifying a situation eliciting a bad mood or emotion (e.g., turning down a loud radio or TV)

__46. talking about your feelings with someone

__47. imagining a pleasant experience to offset a negative feeling

__48. working on a hobby

__49. thinking of good things you have done

__50. actively avoiding situations that depress you

__51. taking action to prevent things that depress you from taking place

__52. doing things at which you are good in order to help you feel better about yourself

__53. helping others in need of help to help you overcome a feeling of depression.

**In using some strategy to keep in touch with, sort out or regulate your moods or emotions, how often do you do the following things? Use this scale to show your responses:**

*I never do this*          *I always do this*

      *1*    *2*    *3*    *4*    *5*    *6*    *7*

__54. checking to make sure that you are properly using the strategy

__55. checking to ensure that the strategy you are using is having its desired effect

__56. adjusting your behavior to better use the strategy

__57. switching to a more effective strategy if you notice that the one you are using is not working well.

# APPENDIX E

## Five Component Scale of Academic Self-Regulation (FCSAR) and Self-Regulated Transfer Scale (SRTS)

### Five-Component Scale of Academic Self-Regulation
(From Martinez-Pons, 2000)

Use this scale to show HOW MANY OF YOUR FAVORITE PASTIMES (hobbies, games, being with friends, watching TV, movies etc.) you are willing to give up to accomplish the following when doing your academic work:

| *none of my* *favorite pastimes* 1 | *some of my* *favorite pastimes* 2 | *a few of my* *favorite pastimes* 3 | *many of my* *favorite pastimes* 4 | *as many of my* *favorite pastimes* *as necessary* 5 |
|---|---|---|---|---|

1. getting some idea of what the material is about
2. meeting the school's passing requirements
3. mastering the material so you can get high grades in school
4. mastering the material so you can apply it to other areas of your life and your academic work

**5. Use this scale to show the amount of effort you typically put into your academic work:**
*1* = not enough effort to accomplish much of anything
*2* = just enough effort to say I tried
*3* = just enough effort to get some idea of what the material is about
*4* = just enough effort to meet the school's passing requirements
*5* = enough effort to get high grades in school

6 = all the effort necessary to master the material so I can apply it to other academic work
7 = all the effort necessary to master the material so I can apply it to my life even out of school

**Use this scale to show the extent to which you agree with the following statements:**
*completely disagree          completely agree*
   1     2     3     4     5     6     7

6. When doing my academic work, I always set goals to guide in my efforts

**Whenever I set goals for doing my academic work, I . . .**
7. make sure that the goals I set for myself involve objectives I have not yet attained, rather than things I have already achieved.
8. check with others (parents, teachers) to make sure that the goals I set for myself are realistic.
9. set goals that are so clear that I can describe them to someone else without difficulty.
10. set goals for myself that go beyond what I have already achieved.
11. set goals that present me with a challenge.
12. check with others (parents, teachers) to make sure that the goals I set for myself are clear.
13. give myself plenty of time to achieve the goals I set for myself.
14. set goals that I think I have a good chance of achieving.
15. check with others (parents, teachers) to make sure that I give myself enough time to work on the goals I set for myself.
16. am able to clearly distinguish my academic goals from one another.
17. check with others (parents, teachers) to make sure that my goals involve objectives that I have not yet attained.
18. make sure that the number of goals I set for myself is manageable.
19. try to organize the goals I set for myself so that attaining one makes it easy to attain another.
20. set a definite deadline (date, time) for reaching each goal I set for myself.
21. can't make sense from one day to the next of the goals I set for myself.

**Some students use the following strategies to perform their academic work, while others prefer not to use strategies such as these. How often do *you* use the strategies listed to perform your academic work? Use this scale to show your responses:**

| | *almost* | | | *much* | *almost* | |
|---|---|---|---|---|---|---|
| *never* | *never* | *sometimes* | *frequently* | *of the time* | *all the time* | *all the time* |
| 1 | 2 | 3 | 4 | 5 | 6 | 7 |

22. getting your teachers to help you when you get stuck on academic work
23. getting other students to help you when you get stuck on academic work
24. getting adults to help you when you get stuck on academic work
25. getting a friend to help you when you get stuck on academic work
26. motivating yourself to do your academic work when you find the material difficult
27. motivating yourself to do your academic work when you find the material boring
28. motivating yourself to do your academic work when you are tired or fatigued
29. motivating yourself to do your academic work when there are other interesting things to do
30. taking notes of class instruction
31. using the library to get information for class assignments
32. planning your academic work
33. organizing your academic work
34. rehearsing to remember information presented in class or textbooks

35. arranging a place to study without distractions
36. taking steps to be able to continue with your academic work when you find the material very hard
37. taking steps to be able to continue with your academic work when you find the material very boring
38. taking steps to be able to continue with your academic work when you are tired or fatigued
39. taking steps to continue with your academic work when there are other interesting things to do

**When using a strategy such as note taking or underlining to do your academic work, how often do you do the following things? Use this scale to show your responses:**

| *almost* | | | | *much* | *almost* | |
|---|---|---|---|---|---|---|
| *never* | *never* | *sometimes* | *frequently* | *of the time* | *all the time* | *all the time* |
| *1* | *2* | *3* | *4* | *5* | *6* | *7* |

40. checking to see if you are performing the strategy in the way it's supposed to be carried out
41. having alternative strategies available in case the one you use does not work
42. comparing your performance with that of others to check to see if you are performing the strategy in the way it's supposed to be carried out
43. checking your work to see if the strategy is having its desired effect
44. comparing the strategy to other methods to see which is more effective
45. keeping records of your performance so you can see how much progress you are making
46. trying out chapter-end problems in textbooks to see how well you have mastered the material
47. taking old tests to see how well you know the material
48. adjusting your behavior as necessary to better use the strategy
49. switching to a more effective strategy when the one you are using is not working
50. reviewing your answers on a test to see what mistakes you have made, if any
51. determining what you did wrong when you find you have not succeeded in mastering the material
52. taking action to rectify the reason for whatever mistakes you have identified
53. checking to make sure you have rectified the mistake
54. rewarding yourself for correcting the mistake

## Self-Regulated Transfer Scale
### (From Martinez-Pons, 2000)

**Use this scale to show the extent to which you agree with the following statements:**

| *completely disagree* | | | | | | *completely agree* |
|---|---|---|---|---|---|---|
| *1* | *2* | *3* | *4* | *5* | *6* | *7* |

**Whenever I find that I have to master a novel task such as learning something new or doing something new at work, I**
1. analyze the situation to see how much of what I already know I can use to help me in mastering the task.
2. analyze the task to see how much of it requires new learning on my part in order for me to master it.
3. combine and use previously learned material to help me in mastering the task.
4. acquire new skills as necessary to help me in mastering the task.
5. combine and use newly acquired skills to help me in mastering the task.
6. test myself to see if what I am doing is helping me in mastering the task.
7. change my behavior if necessary to help me in mastering the task.

# APPENDIX F

---

## Self-Report Questionnaire of Student Mental Efficiency and Academic Performance

**1. Compared to other college students, how quickly are you able to master new academic material?**

*1 = Much more slowly than other students*
*2 = A little more slowly than other students*
*3 = About as quickly as other students*
*4 = A little more quickly than other students*
*5 = Much more quickly than other students*

**2. Compared to other college students, how well can you remember academic material you learn?**

*1 = Much worse than other students*
*2 = A little worse than other students*
*3 = About the same as other students*
*4 = A little better than other students*
*5 = Much better than other students*

**3. Compared to other college students, how extensively can you utilize academic material you learn?**

*1 = Much less extensively than other students*
*2 = A little less extensively than other students*
*3 = About the same as other students*
*4 = A little more extensively than other students*
*5 = Much more extensively than other students*

**4. Compared to other college students, how much difficulty do you think you usually experience with your academic work?**

*1 = Much more difficulty than other students*

*2 = A little more difficulty than other students*

*3 = About the same level of difficulty as other students*

*4 = A little less difficulty than other students*

*5 = Much less difficulty than other students*

**5. Compared to other college students, how well would you say you are doing academically?**

*1 = I would have to make a great effort to do as well as others*

*2 = I would have to make some effort to do as well as others*

*3 = I don't need to make any effort to do as well as others*

*4 = Others would have to make some effort to do as well as I*

*5 = Others would have to make a great effort to do as well as I*

# APPENDIX G

## Self-Report Questionnaire of Student Class Participation Skills

**Use the following scale to indicate how well you can perform the following tasks:**

*1 = I don't know how to do this at all*

*2 = I know a little about how to do this but I need to further develop my skills so I can do it with full confidence*

*3 = I can do this well if no unforeseen difficulties arise*

*4 = I can do this well, and I can overcome any unforeseen difficulties that may arise as I try to do it*

**In preparation for a class discussion:**

__1. Conducting computer-based literature reviews

__2. Conducting hard copy catalogue-based literature reviews

__3. Reading, interpreting, and evaluating scholarly material

__4. Conducting and interpreting personal observations of events around you

__5. Recalling and interpreting personal experiences

__6. Conceptually integrating information gathered through readings, observations, and personal experiences in preparation for the discussion

**During a class discussion:**

__7. Clearly expressing a position on some issue

__8. Arguing a point while maintaining emotional control

__9. Expressing an opinion without offending others

__10. Understanding what someone else is saying

__11. Assessing the validity of what someone else says

__12. Assessing what someone else says for relevance to a topic for discussion
__13. Collaborating with others to solve a problem or achieve some other end

**Following completion of a class discussion:**
__14. Determining what you have gained from the interaction
__15. Integrating what you have gained from the interaction into a frame of reference for thinking about the subject at hand
__16. Assessing how the discussion has changed your outlook regarding the subject at hand
__17. Applying what you learn in situations different from the learning setting

# APPENDIX H

## Independent Report Questionnaire of Student Class Participation Skills

**Use the following scale to indicate how well this student can perform the following tasks:**

*1 = Does not know how to do this at all*

*2 = Knows a little about how to do this but needs to further develop skills to do it with complete effectiveness*

*3 = Can do this well if no unforeseen difficulties arise*

*4 = Can do this well, and can overcome any unforeseen difficulties that may arise as he or she tries to do it*

**In preparation for a class discussion:**

__1. Conducting computer-based literature reviews

__2. Conducting hard copy catalogue-based literature reviews

__3. Reading, interpreting, and evaluating scholarly material

__4. Conducting and interpreting personal observations of events around him or her

__5. Recalling and interpreting personal experiences

__6. Conceptually integrating information gathered through readings, observations, and personal experiences in preparation for the discussion

**During a class discussion:**

__7. Clearly expressing a position on some issue

__8. Arguing a point while maintaining emotional control

__9. Expressing an opinion without offending others

__10. Understanding what someone else is saying

__11. Assessing the validity of what someone else says

__12. Assessing what someone else says for relevance to a topic for discussion
__13. Collaborating with others to solve a problem or achieve some other end

**Following completion of a class discussion:**
__14. Determining what you have gained from the interaction
__15. Integrating what you have gained from the interaction into a frame of reference for thinking about the subject at hand
__16. Assessing how the discussion has changed your outlook regarding the subject at hand
__17. Applying what you learn in situations different from the learning setting

# APPENDIX I

## Self-Report Questionnaire of Instructor Readiness Level

**Use this scale to indicate how well you can guide students in their performance of the following tasks:**

*1 = I cannot help students to do this*

*2 = I know a little about how to help students do this but I need to further develop my skills so I can do it with full confidence*

*3 = I can help students to do this if no unforeseen difficulties arise*

*4 = I can help students to do this, and I can overcome any unforeseen difficulties that may arise as I try to do it*

**Guiding students in their preparation for class work as they attempt to . . .**

\_\_1. conduct electronic and non-electronic literature reviews

\_\_2. read, interpret, and evaluate technical theoretical and research material

\_\_3. conduct, interpret, and conceptually integrate controlled observations of events in their lives

\_\_4. recall, interpret, and conceptually integrate personal experiences

\_\_5. integrate information gathered from readings, observations, and personal experiences to prepare for a class discussion

**Guiding students in their participation in class discussion as they attempt to . . .**

\_\_6. express a position on some issue

\_\_7. express an opinion without offending another person

\_\_8. understand what someone else is saying

\_\_9. assess what someone else says for validity

__10. argue a point without losing emotional control
__11. work in a group to solve a problem or achieve some other end
__12. argue a point with emotional aplomb
__13. keep track of what others are saying
__14. integrate key discussion points into a cohesive whole

**Guiding students in their capitalization on the learning experience as they attempt to . . .**
__15. determine what they have gained from the interaction
__16. integrate learned material into a frame of reference for thinking about the subject at hand
__17. assess how the discussion has changed their outlook regarding the subject at hand
__18. apply what they learn in situations different from the learning setting

**Use this scale to indicate how well you rate yourself on the following areas of teaching:**
*1 = poor*
*2 = below average*
*3 = average*
*4 = above average*
*5 = superior*

__19. Enthusiasm for the topic at hand
__20. Enthusiasm for teaching
__21. Willingness to apply principles of instruction to the teaching-learning effort
__22. Willingness to devote the time and effort necessary to overcome obstacles in the process of instruction
__23. Systematic organization of subject matter
__24. Speaking ability
__25. Ability to explain clearly
__26. Ability to encourage thought
__27. Fairness in grading tests
__28. Tolerance toward student disagreement
__29. Expert knowledge of subject
__30. Sympathetic attitude toward students
__31. Enthusiastic attitude toward subject
__32. Pleasing personality
__33. Spending any time and effort necessary to overcome difficulties you encounter in your work
__34. How long do you intend to continue working as an instructor? Use this scale to show your response:

*Will leave this field*      *Will never leave teaching (will*
*as soon as possible*         *retire as an instructor)*
     *1   2   3   4   5   6   7*

__35. In general, how committed do you feel to your work as an instructor? Use this scale to show your response:

*Not at all committed*      *Extremely committed*
     *1   2   3   4   5   6   7*

# APPENDIX J

## The Course Syllabus

As a minimum, the course syllabus should contain the following items of information:

1. Course title
2. Office hours, office room and telephone numbers
3. Remediation procedures to be used, if any
4. College-catalogue description including prerequisites and co-requisites
5. Objectives of the course
6. Preparation to meet the objectives
7. Assessment methodology
8. Testing policy
9. Unit Schedule
10. Reading schedule
11. Bibliography

The following is a sample course syllabus.

### *Introduction to Educational Research*
Office hours by appointment: 3–5:30 PM, Mon & Wed

Educational Research as applied to analysis of teacher/learner behavior. Use of educational research techniques including exploratory (diagnostic) techniques, to analyze functioning of teachers in urban schools with children of diverse abilities and economic and cultural backgrounds.

### Objectives

This course is designed to familiarize the student with contemporary research methodology in education. At the end of this course, the student will be able to

1.  select a topic for research in education, and focus the problem for investigation;
2.  review the theoretical literature to identify key variables and conceptual frameworks relevant to the problem;
3.  develop a hypothetical model to facilitate the investigation;
4.  develop research questions based on which the problem can be systematically investigated;
5.  review the research literature to generate hypotheses for addressing the research questions; and using contemporary research methodology, design an investigation to test the hypotheses.

The student will demonstrate competencies in these areas by a) passing mid-term and end-of-course pencil-and-paper tests in the area of educational research, each with at least 80 percent accuracy; b) presenting preliminary findings of a review of the literature in an area of the student's choice; c) submitting a typed research proposal, in outline form, in a topic of the student's choice; and d) orally defending the research proposal. The student will prepare to meet these objectives through attendance at lectures, collaborative learning and other class activities, and readings. The final grade will be determined as follows:

¼ mid-term exam
¼ final exam
¼ research proposal and proposal's oral defense
¼ class participation: 95% attendance (3 late arrivals will count as one absence); professional conduct in class; contribution to class discussions and participation in collaborative learning activities; and completion of study assignments

**Schedule for Spring 2002**

| *Unit* | *Topic (Text Page Readings)* |
|---|---|
| 1 | Introduction to research (1–21) |
| 2 | Identification of a research problem area in education/ Focusing the research topic (75–84) |
| 3 | Review of the literature for theory: Variables and their relationships involved in the problem/Types of variables/ Library orientation 21–26) |
| 4 | Development of theoretical model/Structural integrity and instrumental strength of the theoretical model/Derivation of research questions from the theoretical model (84–98) |
| 5 | Review of the literature for research relative to research questions: Instrumental validity, validity of methods and procedures, validity of data analysis methods, validity of conclusions (102–104) |
| 6 | Development of the hypotheses (105–106) |
| 7 | Mid-term exam |
| 8 | Empirical validity of the theoretical model I: Explanatory/ predictive power (106–107) |
| 9 | Empirical validity of the theoretical model II: Parsimony and data fit (109–110) |
| 10 | Empirical validity, sampling and method of data generation (110–120) |
| 11 | Empirical validity and method of data analysis I: Scales of measurement (26–30) |
| 12 | Empirical validity and method of data analysis II: Central tendency/Variability/Data distribution (54–61) |
| 13 | Empirical validity and method of data analysis III: Review of 4 types of research questions (100–102) |
| 14 | Empirical validity and method of data analysis IV: Descriptive and inferential statistics/ Selecting the appropriate statistical procedure/Parametric and non-parametric statistics (61–74) |
| 15 | Review, individual consultations |
| 16 | Research proposal due in |
| 17 | Final exam as scheduled |

**Text**

Martinez-Pons, M. (1996). *Research in the social sciences and education: Principles and process.* Lanham, MD: University Press of America, Inc. Continuum.

# APPENDIX K

## Application of Learned Material

When the learner applies what he or she has learned, he or she does so in three steps. He or she:

1. Notes the demands of the task at hand.
2. Recalls acquired material appropriate to the task's demands.
3. Brings the material to bear on the task.

The student can apply what he or she has learned in one of two ways: to the original task at a time subsequent to his or her acquiring the material, and to tasks different from that involved in the acquisition of the material. In addition, he or she can apply the material in the same context in which he or she has acquired it, or he or she can apply it in a context different from that in which he or she has attained it. Figure K.1 shows interactions between the task and context dimensions of application—with implications for the level of difficulty likely to arise as the person attempts to apply learned material.

| Task | Context | |
|---|---|---|
| | **Initial** | **New** |
| **Initial** | 1 | 2 |
| **New** | 3 | 4 |

**Figure K1. Task and Context Dimensions of Application**

Cell 1 in Figure K.1 refers to the enactment of some mastered affective, cognitive, or psychomotor process with the same task and within the same context as that in which the learner has attained the process. For example, having demonstrated at midpoint in a class session that he or she has learned the rule for addition of simple fractions by solving a fraction problem (for example, 1/5 + 1/3), a student can be called upon to solve the same problem at the end of the class session. This level of application requires recognition that the task at hand is the same as before, and the recall of the applicable process to be enacted.

Cell 2 in Figure K.1 refers to the enactment of some mastered affective, cognitive, or psychomotor process with the initial task but within a context different from that in which the learner has attained the process. For example, having demonstrated at the beginning of a class session mastery of the rule for addition of simple fractions by solving the above problem (i.e., 1/5 + 1/3), the student can be called upon to solve the same problem next day, in a different classroom, with a different teacher in attendance. This level of application requires overcoming of distractions involved in contextual variation, recognition of the task as the same as before, and the recall of the applicable process to be enacted.

Cell 3 in Figure K.1 refers to the enactment of some mastered affective, cognitive, or psychomotor process with a different task within the same context as that in which the learner attained the process. For example, at the end of the class session, the above student would use the rule for adding simple fractions he or she learned earlier to solve the following problem: 1/7 + 1/6. This level of application requires the abstraction of that which the novel and original tasks share in common and recall of the applicable process to be enacted.

Cell 4 in Figure K.1 refers to the enactment of some mastered affective, cognitive, or psychomotor process with a different task and within a context different from that in which the learner attained the process. For example, for the above student, on a different day, in a different classroom, with a different teacher in charge, the student would use the same rule to solve the following problem: 1/8 + 2/7. This level of application requires overcoming of distractions associated with contextual variation, the abstraction of that which the novel and original tasks share in common, and recall of the relevant process to be enacted.

# References

Anastasi, A. (1982) *Psychological testing (5th ed.)*. New York: Macmillan.

d'Apollonia, S. and Abrami, P. C. (1997) Navigating student ratings of instruction. *American Psychologist*, 52, 1198–208.

Archer, J., Cantwell, R. and Bourke, S. (1999) Coping at university: an examination of achievement, motivation, self-regulation, confidence, and method of entry. *Higher Education Research and Development*, 18, 31–54.

Aubrecht, J. D. (1979) *Are student ratings of teacher effectiveness valid? Idea Paper No. 2*. Manhattan, KS: Kansas State University, Center for Faculty Evaluation and Development.

Bandura, A. (1977a) *Social learning theory*. Englewood Cliffs, NJ: Prentice-Hall.

Bandura, A. (1977b) Self-efficacy: Toward a unifying theory of behavioral change. *Psychological Review*, 84, 191–215.

Bandura, A. (1986) *Social foundations of thought and action*. Englewood Cliffs, NJ: Prentice-Hall.

Bandura, A. (1989a) *Multidimensional scales of perceived self-efficacy (MSPS)*. Unpublished manuscript.

Bandura, A. (1989b) Regulation of cognitive processes through perceived self-efficacy. *Developmental Psychology*, 25, 729–35.

Bangura, A. K. (1994) *The focus-group approach as an alternative for collecting faculty evaluation data to improve teaching.* Paper presented at the Center for Educational Development and Assessment Conference on Faculty Evaluation, San Juan, Puerto Rico.

Barnett, J. E. (2000) Self-regulated reading and test preparation among college students. *Journal of College Reading and Learning*, 31, 42–53.

Baron, A. (1999) *Bud's easy research paper computer manual: 10 steps to an A+ paper.* New York: Lawrence House Publishers.

Bentler, P. M. and Bonnett, D. G. (1980) Significance tests and goodness of fit in the analysis of covariance matrices. *Psychological Bulletin*, 88, 588–606.

Berliner, D. C. and Calfee, R. C. (1998) *Handbook of educational psychology.* New York: Macmillan.

Biehler, R. F. and Snowman, J. (1986) *Psychology applied to teaching.* Boston: Houghton Mifflin Company.

Bloom, B. S., Englehart, M. D., Furst, E. J., Hill, W. H. and Krathwohl, D. R. (1956) *Taxonomy of educational objectives, Handbook I: Cognitive domain.* New York: Longmans Green.

Bolig, E. E. and Day, J. D. (1993) Dynamic assessment and giftedness: The promise of assessing training responsiveness. *Roeper Review*, 16, 110–13.

Callahan, J. F., Clark, L. H. and Kellough, R. D. (1998) *Teaching in the middle and secondary schools.* Upper Saddle River, NJ: Merrill/ Prentice Hall.

Campbell, D. T. and Stanley, J. C. (1963) Experimental and quasi-experimental designs for research on teaching. In N. L. Gage (ed.), *Handbook of research on Teaching* (pp. 171–246). Chicago: Rand McNally.

Carlson, R. (1989) *Vitae Scholasticae*, 8.

Carré, P. (1998) *Adult education today.* Invited address delivered at the Program in Educational Psychology of the Graduate School and University Center of the City University of New York.

Cashin, W. E. (1995) *Student ratings of teaching: the research revisited. IDEA Paper No. 32.*

Ceci, S. J. and Roazzi, A. (1994) The effects of context on cognition: Postcards from Brazil. In R. J. Sternberg and R. K. Wagner (eds), *Mind in context.* New York: Cambridge University Press.

Charles, B. (1978) Some limits to the validity and usefulness of student ratings of teachers: An argument for caution. *Educational Research Quarterly*, 3, 12–27.

Childs, R. A. (1989) *Constructing classroom achievement tests.* ERIC Digest. ED315426.

Cohen, J. (1960) A coefficient of agreement for nominal scales. *Educational and Psychological Measurement*, 20, 37–46.

Cohen, P. A. and McKeachie, W. J. (1980) The role of colleagues in the evaluation of college teaching. *Improving college and university teaching*, 28, 147–54.

Collins, A., Brown, J. S. and Newman, S. E. (1989) Cognitive apprenticeship: Teaching the crafts of reading, writing, and mathematics. In L. B. Resnick (ed.), *Knowing, learning, and instruction: Essays in honor of Robert Glaser*. Hillsdale, NJ: Erlbaum.

Mindscape (1995) *Complete reference library*. Novato, CA: Author.

Crow, L. D. and Crow, A. (1954) *Educational psychology*. New York: American Book Company.

Davis, G. A. (1983) *Educational psychology: Theory and practice*. New York: Random House.

Derry, S. and Lesgold, A. (1998) Toward a situated social practice model for instructional design. In D. C. Berliner and R. C. Calfee (eds.), *Handbook of educational psychology*. New York: Macmillan.

Draves, W. A. *How to teach adults*. Manhattan, Kansas: The Learning Resources Network (LERN).

Dwyer, C. A. and Stufflebeam, D. (1996) Teacher evaluation. In D. C. Berliner and R. C. Calfee (eds), *Handbook of Educational Psychology*. New York: Macmillan.

Ehrlich, E. H. (1963) *How to study better and get higher marks*. New York: Bantam Books.

Elias, J. L. and Merriam, S. (1980) *Philosophical foundations of adult education*. Malabar, FL: Robert E. Krieger Publishing Company.

Ericsson, K. A. and Charnes, N. (1994) Expert performance. *American Psychologist*, 49, 725–47.

Fox, D. J. (1969) The research process in education. New York: Holr, Rinehar and Boyd.

Furst, E. J. (1981) Bloom's taxonomy of educational objectives for the cognitive domain: philosophical and educational issues. *Review of Educational Research*, 51, 441–53.

Gabriel, R. M., Anderson, B. L., Benson, G., Gordon, S., Hill, R., Pfannenstiel, J. and Stonehill, R. M. (1985) *Studying the sustained achievement of Chapter 1 students*. Washington, DC: US Department of Education.

Gaff, J. G. and Pruitt-Logan, A. S. (1998) Preparing college faculty. *New Directions for Higher Education*, 26, 77–86.

Gage, N. L. and Berliner, D. C. (1984) *Educational psychology (3rd ed.)*. Boston: Houghton Mifflin Company.

Gagné, R. M. (1964) The implications of instructional objectives for learning. In C. M. Lindvall (ed.), *Defining educational objectives*. Pittsburgh: University of Pittsburgh Press.

Gagné, R. M. (1985) *The conditions of learning (4th ed.)*. New York: Holt.

Goleman, D. (1995) *Emotional intelligence*. New York: Bantam Books.

Goodman, L. A. and Kruskal, W. H. (1954) Measures of association for cross classifications. *Journal of the American Statistical Association*, 49, 732–64.

Griffin, M. L. (2002) *Using critical incidents to facilitate and assess pre-service teachers' growth in reflective and critical thinking*. Paper presented at the American Association for Higher Education 2002 Assessment Conference.

Gronlund, N. E. (1978) *Stating objectives for classroom instruction (2nd ed.)*. New York: Macmillan.

Hall, C., Lindzey, G. and Campbell, J. B. (1988) *Theories of personality*. New York: John Wiley.

Hilgard, J. R. (1996) Educational psychology. In D. C. Berliner and R. C. Calfee (eds), *Handbook of educational psychology*. New York: Macmillan.

Houghton Mifflin Company *The American Heritage Dictionary of the English language (4th ed.)* (2000) New York.

Houle, C. O. (1974) The changing goals of education in the perspective of lifelong Learning. *International Review of Education*, 20, 430–46.

Jampole, E. S. (1990) *Effects of imagery training on the creative writing of academically gifted elementary students*. Paper presented at the 40th Annual Meeting of the National Reading Conference.

Jensen, A. (1985) *Bias in mental testing*. New York: The Free Press.

Judd, C. H. (1916) *Psychology of high-school subjects*. Boston: Guinnes.

Kallos, D. and Lundgren, U. P. (1975) Educational psychology: Its scope and limits. *British Journal of Educational Psychology*, 45, 111–21.

Kaufman, B. and Madden, J. M. (1980) *The development of behaviorally anchored rating scales for student evaluation of college teaching effectiveness*. Paper presented at the 51st Annual Meeting of the Eastern Psychological Association.

Kibler, R. J., Barker, L. L. and Miles, D. T. (1970) *Behavioral objectives and instruction*. Boston: Allyn and Bacon.

Kidd, J. R. (1980) Training and research – The 1980s. *NSPI Journal*, 14, 8–10.

Knowles, M. S. (1970) *The modern practice of adult education; andragogy versus pedagogy*. New York: The Association Press.

Knowles, M. S. (1973) *The adult learner: a neglected species*. Houston, TX: Gulf Publishing Company.

Knowles, M. S. (1980) *The modern practice of adult education; from pedagogy to adult education*. New York: The Association Press.

Knowles, M. S., Holton, E. F. III and Swanson, R. A. (1998) *The adult learner. The definitive classic in adult education and human resource development (5th ed.)*. Houston, TX: Gulf Publishing Company, Book Division.

Knudson, R. E. (1998) College students' writing: An assessment of competence. *Journal of Experimental Education*, 92, 13–20.

Krathwohl, D., Bloom, B. S. and Masia, B. (1964) *Taxonomy of educational objectives. Handbook II: Affective domain*. New York: McKay.

Kropp, R. P. and Stoker, H. W. (1966). *The construction and validation of tests of the cognitive processes as described in the taxonomy of educational objectives*. Florida State University, Institute of Human Learning and Department of Educational Research and Testing: ERIC Accession Number ED 010044.

Lang, T. (1998) *An overview of four futures methodologies*. Retrieved by Shirley King on January 29, 1999 from the World Wide Web: http:// www.soc.hamaii.edu/~future/j7/LANG.html.

Ley, K. and Young, D. B. (1998) Self-regulation behaviors in underprepared (developmental) and regular admission college students. *Contemporary Educational Psychology*, 23, 42–64.

Linn, R. L., Baker, E. L. and Dunbar, S. B. (1991) Complex, performance-based assessment: Expectations and validation criteria. *Educational Researcher*, 20, 15–21.

Madaus, G. F., Woods, E. M. and Nutall, R. L. (1973) A causal model analysis of Bloom's taxonomy. *American Educational Research Journal*, 10, 253–62.

Mager, R. F. (1962) *Preparing instructional objectives*. Palo Alto, CA: Fearon Publishers.

Martinez-Pons, M. (1996) Test of a model of parental inducement of academic self-regulation. *The Journal of Experimental Education*, 64, 213–27.

Martinez-Pons, M. (1997) *Research in the social sciences and education:*

*Principles and process.* Lanham, MD: University Press of America.

Martinez-Pons, M. (1997–1998) The relation of emotional intelligence with selected areas of personal functioning. *Imagination, Cognition and Personality*, 17, 3–14.

Martinez-Pons, M. (1998) Grounded theory development of a teacher-oriented model of mental ability. *The Journal of Secondary Gifted Education*, 9, 195–206.

Martinez-Pons, M. (1998–1999) Parental inducement of emotional intelligence. *Imagination, Cognition and Personality*, 18, 3–23.

Martinez-Pons, M. (1999) Statistics in modern research. Applications in the social sciences and education. Lanham, MD: University Press of America.

Martinez-Pons, M. (1999–2000) Emotional intelligence as a self-regulatory process: A social cognitive view. *Imagination, Cognition and Personality*, 19, 331–50.

Martinez-Pons, M. (2000) *Transfer as a self-regulatory process: Implications for self-instruction in adult education.* Paper given at the Second Royaumont Symposium on Self-Learning, Paris.

Martinez-Pons, M. (2001) *The psychology of teaching and learning: A three-step approach.* London: Continuum.

Martinez-Pons, M., Rosello, J. and Tempestini, M. (1995) *Multiple roles and psychological functioning in two cultures.* Paper presented at the 35th Annual Meeting of the New England Psychological Association.

Miller, W. G., Snowman, J. and O'Hara, T. (1979) Application of alternative statistical techniques to examine the hierarchical ordering in Bloom's taxonomy. *American Educational Research Journal*, 16, 241–8.

Mindscape (1995) *Complete reference library.* Novato, CA.

Mohring, P. M. (1989) *Andragogy and pedagogy: A comment on their erroneous usage. Training and Development Research Center project number twenty-nine.* Resources in Education (RIE): ERIC Accession Number ED305509.

Morrow, J. R. (1977) Some statistics regarding the reliability and validity of student ratings of teachers. *Research Quarterly*, 48, 372–5.

Nel, J. (1990) *University response to the educational needs of adults: Evidence from the past.* Paper presented at the 39th Annual Meeting of the American Association for Adult and Continuing Education.

New York State Education Department (1999) *Liberal Arts and Science Test (LAST).* New York.

Orange, C. (1999) Using peer modeling to teach self-regulation. *The Journal of Experimental Education*, 68, 21–38.

Osgood, Ann F. and York, Paula A. (1992) *Faculty teacher training at the post-secondary level*. Northern Maine Technical College: ERIC Accession Number ED362511.

Owen, S. A. (1976) *The validity of student ratings: a critique*. Paper presented at the Annual Meeting of the National Council on Measurement in Education, San Francisco, California.

Peterson, C., Marer, S. F. and Seligman, M. E. P. (1993) *Learned helplessness: A theory for the age of personal control*. New York: Oxford University Press.

Platt, M. (1993) What student evaluations teach. *Perspectives in Political Science*, 22 (1), 29–40.

Pressley, M. and McCormick, C. (1995) *Advanced educational psychology for educators, researchers, and policymakers*. New York: HarperCollins.

Rachal, J. R. (1994) Andragogical and pedagogical methods compared: a review of the experimental literature. Resources in Education (RIE) AN: ERIC Accession Number ED380566.

Reigh, L. and Waggoner, M. D. (1995) *Collaborative peer review: The role of faculty in improving college teaching*. Washington, DC: Office of Educational Research and Improvement.

Ruskai, M. B. (1996) Evaluating student evaluations. *Notices of The American Mathematical Society*, 44(3), 308.

Salovey, P. and Meyer, J. D. (1989) Emotional intelligence. *Imagination, Cognition and Personality*, 9, 185–211.

Salovey, P., Meyer, J. D., Goldman, S. L., Turvey, C. and Palfai, T. (1995) Emotional attention, clarity and repair: Exploring emotional intelligence using the trait meta-mood scale. In J. W. Pennebaker (ed.) *Emotion, disclosure, and health*. Washington, D.C.: American Psychological Association.

Savicevic, D. M. (1985) Self-directed education for lifelong education. *International Journal of Lifelong Education*, 4, 285–94.

Savicevic, D. M. (1990) Contemporary trends in adult education research in Yugoslavia. *International Journal of Lifelong Education*, 9, 129–35.

Savicevic, D. M. (1991) Modern conceptions of andragogy: A European framework. *Studies in the Education of Adults*, Vol. 23, 179–201.

Savicevic, D. M. (1996) Universities and adult education in the federal republic of Yugoslavia. *International Journal of University Adult Education*, 35, 88–100.

Savicevic, D. M. (1999) *Adult education: from practice to theory building: studies in pedagogy, andragogy, and gerontagogy.* New York: Peter Lang.

Schapiro, S. R. and Livingston, J. (2000) Dynamic self-regulation: The driving force behind academic achievement. *Innovative Higher Education*, 25, 23–35.

Schunk, D. L. (1991) *Learning theories: An educational perspective.* New York: Macmillan.

Seddon, G. M. (1978) The properties of Bloom's taxonomy of educational objectives for the cognitive domain. *Review of Educational Research*, 48, 303–3.

Shanley, D., Martinez-Pons, M. and Rubal-Lopez, A. (1999) *Self-regulation of multiple social roles, study skills, and performance on the New York state teacher certification examination.* Paper presented at the 39th annual meeting of the New England Psychological Association, Hartford, Connecticut.

Shulman, L. S. and Quinlan, K. M. (1998) The comparative psychology of school subjects. In D. C. Berliner and R. C. Calfee (eds), *Handbook of educational psychology.* New York: Macmillan.

Simpson, E. J. (1972) *The classification of educational objectives: Psychomotor domain.* Urbana, IL: University of Illinois Press.

Skinner, B. F. (1968) *The technology of teaching.* New York: Appleton-Century-Crofts.

Slavin, R. E. (1985) Team-assisted individualization: Combining cooperative learning and individualized instruction in mathematics. In R. Slavin, S. Shara, S. Kagan, R. H. Lazarowitz, C. Webb, R. Schmuck (eds), *Learning to cooperate, cooperating to learn* (pp. 177–209). New York: Plenum.

Smith, M. C. and Pourchot, T. (eds.) (1998) *Adult learning and development: Perspectives from educational psychology. The educational psychology series.* Mahwah, NJ: Lawrence Erlbaum Associates, Inc.

Smith, R. M., Neisworth, J. T. and Greer, J. G. (1978) *Evaluating educational environments.* Columbus, OH: Charles E. Merrill.

Stevens, J. (1996) *Applied multivariate statistics for the social sciences (3rd ed.).* Mahwah, NJ: Lawrence Earlbaum Associates.

Strage, Amy A. (1998) Family context variables and the development of self-regulation in college students. *Adolescence*, 33, 17–31.

Theall, M. and Franklyn, J. (1991). Using student ratings for teaching improvement. *New Directions for Teaching and Learning*, 48, 83–96.

Thompson, G. (1989) The complete adult educator: a reconceptualization of andragogy and pedagogy. *Canadian Journal of University Continuing Education*, 15, 1–12.

Thorndike, E. L. (1903) *Educational psychology*. New York: Science Press.

Tice, E. T. (1997) Educating adults: a matter of balance. *Adult Learning*, 9, 18–21.

Webster, R. E. (1981) *Learning efficiency test (*LET*) manual*. Novato, CA: Academic Therapy Publications.

Weinstein, C. and Palmer, D. R. (1998) *Learning and Study Strategies Inventory*. Clearwater, FL: HandH Publishing.

Williams, J. (1991) *Writing quality teacher-made tests: a handbook for teachers*. Wheaton, MD: Wheaton High School.

Withall, J. (1949) The development of a technique for the measurement of social climate in classrooms. *Journal of Experimental Education*, 17, 347–61.

Zimmerman, B. J. (1989). A social cognitive view of self-regulated academic learning. *Journal of Educational Psychology*, 81, 329–39.

Zimmerman, B. J. and Martinez-Pons, M. (1986) Development of a structured interview for assessing student use of self-regulated learning strategies. *American Educational Research Journal*, 23, 614–28.

# Index